*Published by*
Lambert-Gann Publishing Co., Inc.
P. O. Box O, Pomeroy, Wn. 99347

ISBN 978-0-939093-11-3

*To*

LLEWELLYN GEORGE

Pioneer in American astro-research, who gave me a world-wide audience from 1931 to 1954 in his BULLETINA quarterly; Arthur I. Boreman, publisher of the MERCHANT'S TRADE JOURNAL, who never edited one word from my business trend comments every month from 1933 to 1959; and, to Billy Jones who insisted this material should be printed and published as a heritage to others to expand their success.

## CONTENTS

CHARTS AND MAPS (*Partial List—see Text*)

# PREFACE

The bulk of the material in this edition was published in three brochures copyright 1935 and 1938. A condensation of the third brochure on charting market statistics was issued as one of many market studies while I was an analyst for a New York Stock Exchange firm. This edition comprises all of the original three works with some additional material in order to bridge the three into a continuity plus a number of working examples of methods which apply the principles involved.

Section I offers some introduction to working applications of what I term astro-cycles. The sources are the long established astronomical orbits of the principal planets in that small niche of the Universe which comprises the Solar System of the Earth. For example, applied to cycle cadence is Jupiter and Saturn with their apparent conjunction approximately every 20 years. Many of these planetary cycle applications were original when published in 1934, but since then have been lifted out of context and embraced by publications issued in Calcutta, Hong Kong, London, New York and Los Angeles. The plagiarism is of little importance but the widespread practice has brought to attention the unquestioned validity of the data.

The purpose of the material in Section II was a notebook reference manual to present the salient procedures and elements of astro-cycle applications to mundane affairs. Public psychology, business cycles, the price swings of speculative commodity and stock markets, wars, famines, major weather trends, etc, have innumerable keys to answers by this concept.

Very little of the material has been co-ordinated before in print so that a student might quickly grasp the more significant factors. Separately most of the factors have been generally known but not the why and how of mixing them. Part of this condition has been intentional: why throw to the winds hard won data? There is another side though. Modern society has boxed itself in, painted itself into a dangerous corner. Outwardly it is in great shape in its apparent affluence, mechanical achievements and productive know-how. Actually it is a shell of wasted resources, mountainous debt, galloping inflation, and eroding moral concepts. An Age is at an end which is out of date, primitive and self-righteous with the chest-pounding adage that man is captain of his fate. He may perish unless he gets down to the reality of Natural Law.

Section II contains no pretense of giving all the answers to modern problems. However, it does offer a means to a well-hidden phase of Truth which might lead to a foundation of security for those diligent enough to examine and test the data. That such an approach infuriates those who proudly hold that nature has no design, no purpose and no form of continuity ceased to concern me more than fifty years ago.

A major factor in the workings of Natural Law is cosmic radiation, that enormous vibrational power of the Sun which is reflected, deflected and mixed with the vibrational forces of planets striking the Earth in a constantly varying array. Often it is ponderously stated that none of these vibrations are strong enough to affect a human being. In almost the same breath they talk about the possible uses of solar energy. No matter if proven, or hallowed, or generally accepted as a fact of life it is always easy to find some clown who vehemently disagrees. Perhaps the answer is not the defense of the how and the why, but does it work, does it give results?

In my youth it was generally accepted that the claim electrical signals could be transmitted without wires was a complete hoax, equal only to the idea that man could fly in anything but a balloon. On these two points alone college professors rated as scientific authorities, plus office holders who felt they protected the people, were around giving lectures warning against such idiotic claims.

Here are methods and their working factors of close to a half a century of producing results. It is an esoteric subject; it is not for the average investor who really gets his kicks putting money into an array of stocks and then every day sweating the price movements. Over the years he usually ends up with one winner and ten losers. This material is for the serious winner who has the attitude of a navigator and impersonally obeys his computations. He is not in markets for kicks but for profits.

Section III uses some of the basic factors of Section II and applies them to a system which is a coupling of time and price. It is a simple charting of market prices. It is so simple any change or revision in the basic premises involved destroys its effectiveness. It will not work properly with logarythmic scales, and the dependence on time brooks no shortcuts or distortion in the arithmetic scale.

September 1977 L. J. JENSEN

# Section I

# MAJOR TRENDS IN AMERICAN ECONOMICS

CHAPTER ONE

# THE PROBLEM OF ECONOMIC CAUSATION

The habit of popular thinking lies along the vein that all economic problems are merely debatable theories. All economic affairs are viewed from much the same perspective as religious or political opinions; as something entirely dependent on the particular prejudice which happens to fit the environmental or geographical viewpoint. So it seems strange to suggest that there may be immutable laws that motivate the psychology of masses of people, and that imponderable forces operate in economic affairs without respect for the hopes and ambitions of men. At first glance it might appear that such a postulate should be the source of considerable popular derision, but perhaps only because the field of observation has been studiously ignored in modern times. At any rate, there appear to be several definite forces underlying the ebb and flow of the economic indices.

It is the purpose, in this brochure and the companion volumes of the series, to examine considerable evidence bearing on economic causation. The observations contained in this brochure will deal entirely with the longer or major trends in American economic history. In the search for causes the prime interest will be, not to align the historical events with the coincident statistical business record and dovetail technical results with psychological effects; but to go deeper and attempt to trace those natural causes which appear to motivate the changes in mass psychology and result in given effects. After locating the source or cause we shall then examine the manner in which natural psychological cycles coincide with the cycles of statistical business activity.

In confining popular economic observations to a few of the generalities like supply and demand, costs, available markets and distribution, labor, et cetera, the subject of economics is principally concerned with statistical results and psychological effects. Underlying causes of such phenomena as the business cycle have only been studied in a superficial manner. This will probably continue to be the situation until the search for causes is taken out of the field of statistics and placed in the field of psychology. At present, causes of economic fluctuation are either considered so remote and intangible that they cannot be defined, or else they are discarded as impractical. Economic effects, or rather statistical results, are paramount. We see economic effects all about us; we deal daily in effects, read of them in the news, see them in moving pictures, and hear them from others. Yet in confining all of our economic thinking to effects we are much like the remaining few who believe that the entire place of medicine is to be strictly curative and disregard efforts of anything preventive. Obviously, some approach toward analyzing economic causes is in order, if an economy is to be planned or any estimates are to be taken of the future.

The debatable method of approach to economics, or the study of effects, might be excused by saying the average mind is so confined to narrow habit that a co-ordination of vast principles is impossible. It might be explained from the viewpoint of the doctrine of free-will, which teaches that man is supreme, the source of both his success and his failure, and therefore the complete master of his fate. We might even offer the excuse that mankind is still in that stage of a blundering evolution where economic causes cannot be co-ordinated. But to present such explanations tie up with effects, again ignoring causes.

Basic causes of economic effects are as intangible as life itself. They cannot be located with any of the senses, such as hearing, seeing or tasting. They cannot be weighed by political votes, or religious followers. They cannot be found in laboratory test tubes, the statistical reviews of business activity, security prices, or in the opinions of celebrities. When we search for causes in these sources, we are simply dealing with another phase of economic effects.

We cannot feel, see or taste the radio-frequency power that blankets the earth's atmosphere. Yet its presence can be proven with a radio receiver. It is impossible to sense the force that shifts the ocean, effecting the tides. We have never been able to measure a mother's love for her child, and the attraction and repulsion that occurs between people. The effects are usually obvious to the senses, but never the causes.

Dealing almost exclusively with effects is the human habit. Probably ninety-five per cent of the people spend all of their time trying to change the effects about them. They attempt to change one situation only to meet another. It is often a case of leaving one discomfort or distress for another. Perhaps a scant five per cent of the people realize that to make any constructive change they must first locate a cause. It is in this search for causes that the minority find the seat of power; by locating causes and then applying the power for desired effects.

The basis of all causation in human affairs lies in the laws of vibration in nature. When we step aside from these natural laws we leave the field of causation and turn back to the analysis of effects, or the reflectors of causes. The modern developments in therapy; radio and electronics; sound, both music and noise; light and heat; indicate that all of us are entirely bound up in the laws of vibration. Feelings, and all action are vibrations. The key to our individual psychology, our mass psychology as a nation, and our entire economic life, is bound up with vibration. It is in this field of vibration that we are directing our observation of economic causation, to try and locate the coincident effects which might be generated.

CHAPTER TWO

# THE VIBRATION SPECTRUM

Sound, light and heat are all forms of vibration. Each field has its own spectrum or scale of vibration. Sound is an impulse of air striking the organs of hearing with a perceptible effect. Light is that action wherein objects are made visible. Heat is another force, similar to sound and light, in that it has a rate of vibration also. Each of these natural actions have their spectra occupying niches in the huge vibrational spectrum of nature.

Modern science indicates that all bodies, unless at the absolute zero of temperature—assigned by physicists as minus 273 degrees Centigrade —emit vibrations. Most of these vibrations are not visible to the eye, sensitive to the touch or audible to the ear. The frequencies, or rates of vibration, vary from a few cycles per second to millions of cycles per second and include everything from sound waves to gamma and cosmic rays.

A crude illustration of the huge vibration spectrum may be made by drawing a pencil line about a foot long. At the left end of this line mark an (X). This point illustrates the rate of vibration of the musical note "B," four octaves below middle "C" on the piano scale, or thirty cycles per second. Move to the right on the pencil line about a half inch from (X) and mark (Y). This point represents a frequency of 5,120 cycles per second, the high musical note "E," four octaves above middle "C." As the rate of vibration rises above approximately 16,000 cycles per second—the pitch of some squeaks—it ceases to be audible to the human ear. We take this approximate half inch section on the pencil line to represent the sound spectrum niche of the major vibrational scale.

From the point (Y) move to the right on the pencil line—to establish the beginning of the electro-magnetic spectrum—about three inches, marking the point as (Z). This point represents the beginning of the modern radio spectrum. Moving to the right on the pencil line another three inches will approximate the radio spectrum, this right hand point representing frequencies of about sixty thousand kilocycles and wavelengths of five meters or less.

Again move to the right on the pencil line, after leaving a gap of about an inch to represent the lapping of the short wave radio band and the frequencies of the infra-red and heat rays, the center of which represents the rate of vibration of the color yellow, or approximately a rate of vibration of 500,000,000,000,000 cycles per second. In this spectrum is the frequency range where the human eye is able to directly detect the electro-magnetic vibrations we know as light and color. The eye continues this ability until the rate of vibration increases above that of the color violet.

Move to the right on the pencil line another quarter inch and mark the point (A). This quarter inch section represents the ultra-violet ray spectrum on the edge of the x-ray division. From this point (A) to the extreme right hand end of the pencil line represents the several segments of; first, the x-rays; then the gamma rays; and finally, the cosmic rays. In the spectra of gamma and cosmic rays the frequency is so tremendous that a huge line of figures would be necessary to represent the rate. The wave length at these frequencies is of the order of one ten thousandth of one ten millionth of a millimeter or less.

Observations indicate that the earth's atmosphere is permeated with high frequency radiation of tremendous penetrating power. Although this force is more intense at great heights than at the earth's surface, it is just as intense at night as during the day. At sea level this radiation breaks up about 1.4 atoms in every cubic centimeter of air per second, so it cannot be denied that millions of atoms are broken up in every human body every second. This is the source of distinct biological and in turn, psychological, changes in people. Far more penetrating than any other type of vibration it has been found that the most penetrating portion of these rays will pass through sixteen feet of lead.

It is only very recently that an analysis of the biological and psychological effects of these rays has been attempted by exact science. However, the effect of this energy has been observed by man for centuries.

Simple physics illustrates with a prism how a small segment of sunlight can be separated into the seven primary colors. On the angle of refraction of the sun-rays through the prism depends the particular color in the spectrum. Experiments indicate that a similar type of refraction process occurs through the planets in their relation to the Sun and Earth. Radiation on the surface of the Earth is composed of: first, the rays of the Sun which are refracted by the Earth's magnetism and atmosphere; second, the refracted rays of the Sun, each changed in a particular manner through the angle in which they are reflected from the planets; and, the radiation of each planet. This condition indicates that the frequency of solar radiation is much broader than just the light and heat spectra, covering the entire electro-magnetic spectrum from radio waves to cosmic rays.

We shall now proceed to examine the effects of this radiation in the light of economics and mass psychology.

CHAPTER THREE

# THE SUN SPOT CYCLE

The Sun, as the center of the Earth's little niche in the Universe, is credited with being the source of all of our energy. The Sun is a star, although it is not the largest, or the brightest, or the hottest star, in the Universe. But it is the ruler of the solar system of which the Earth is one unit; and controls the motion of the Earth and all the other planets.

On the surface of the Sun, or its photosphere, often are seen dark spots, some of which are many times larger than the Earth. The occurrence of these spots was noted by the Chinese long before Galileo used his telescope in 1610. Hale found that at its center a Sun-spot has the properties of a huge bar magnet. Researches by Schwabe and then Wolf, which were followed by very systematic observations, show there is an increase and then a decrease in Sun-spot totality with a "regular irregularity" of about 11.2 years. The interval varies in a range of about four years. The movement from maximum to minimum averages about 6.5 years, and the rise from minimum to maximum about 4.6 years.

In the extensive researches involving the business cycle, as indicated in the charted tabulation of the statistics of business activity over a long term of years, there is a distinct relation between the periods of prosperity and depression and the Sun-spot cycle. The work financed by the Harvard committee on research in social sciences has resulted in tracing this correlation from the 17th century South Sea Bubble down to the present year. The last Sun-spot cycle began with a minimum of spots in 1923, a maximum in 1928–1929, and another minimum in 1933–1934. Another maximum point is expected late in 1938. The general averages of Sun-spots for the past 100 years are tabulated on the next page. Current technical and scientific data is obtainable through Science Service, Washington, D. C.

A phenomena of Sun-spots is that the measure of solar radiation in the heat spectrum of vibration shows an increase in the Sun's heat with an increase in the Sun-spot totality. Solar radiation at heat and light frequencies averages close to two horsepower per square meter on the Earth's surface. The solar energy constant is usually taken as 1.94 calories. But when Sun-spots are at a minimum this value changes to about 1.92, and when Sun-spots are near a maximum the value averages 1.96. My conclusion is that this variation in the energy constant affects the mass of humanity biologically and therefore psychologically, in the manner reflected by the rise and fall of the statistics of business activity, or economic energy.

Considerable work has been done in the field of correlating rainfall and the Sun-spot cycle as a clue to factors in long range weather forecasting. The effects of the cycle have been strikingly shown to coincide with tree ring phenomena. It has also been proven there is a coincidence between the amount of ultra-violet radiation and Sun-spots. Even the

TABLE OF SUN-SPOT AVERAGES

| *Year* | *Average* | *Year* | *Average* | *Year* | *Average* |
|---|---|---|---|---|---|
| 1837 | 138.3 | 1871 | 111.2 | 1905 | 63.5 |
| 1838 | 103.2 | 1872 | 101.7 | 1906 | 53.3 |
| 1839 | 85.8 | 1873 | 66.3 | 1907 | 62.0 |
| 1840 | 63.2 | 1874 | 44.7 | 1908 | 48.5 |
| 1841 | 36.8 | 1875 | 17.1 | 1909 | 43.9 |
| 1842 | 24.2 | 1876 | 11.3 | 1910 | 18.6 |
| 1843 | 10.7 | 1877 | 12.3 | 1911 | 5.7 |
| 1844 | 15.0 | 1878 | 3.4 | 1912 | 3.6 |
| 1845 | 40.1 | 1879 | 6.0 | 1913 | 1.4 |
| 1846 | 61.5 | 1880 | 32.3 | 1914 | 9.6 |
| 1847 | 98.5 | 1881 | 54.3 | 1915 | 47.4 |
| 1848 | 124.3 | 1882 | 59.7 | 1916 | 55.4 |
| 1849 | 95.9 | 1883 | 63.7 | 1917 | 103.9 |
| 1850 | 66.5 | 1884 | 63.5 | 1918 | 80.6 |
| 1851 | 64.5 | 1885 | 52.2 | 1919 | 63.6 |
| 1852 | 54.2 | 1886 | 25.4 | 1920 | 38.7 |
| 1853 | 39.0 | 1887 | 13.1 | 1921 | 24.7 |
| 1854 | 20.6 | 1888 | 6.8 | 1922 | 14.7 |
| 1855 | 6.7 | 1889 | 6.3 | 1923 | 5.8 |
| 1856 | 4.3 | 1890 | 7.1 | 1924 | 16.7 |
| 1857 | 22.8 | 1891 | 35.6 | 1925 | 44.3 |
| 1858 | 54.8 | 1892 | 73.0 | 1926 | 63.9 |
| 1859 | 93.8 | 1893 | 84.9 | 1927 | 68.5 |
| 1859 | 93.8 | 1893 | 84.9 | 1927 | 68.5 |
| 1860 | 95.7 | 1894 | 78.0 | 1928 | 77.8 |
| 1861 | 77.2 | 1895 | 64.0 | 1929 | 65.0 |
| 1862 | 59.1 | 1896 | 41.8 | 1930 | 35.7 |
| 1863 | 44.0 | 1897 | 26.2 | 1931 | 21.2 |
| 1864 | 47.0 | 1898 | 26.7 | 1932 | 11.1 |
| 1865 | 30.5 | 1899 | 12.1 | 1933 | 5.7 |
| 1866 | 16.3 | 1900 | 9.5 | 1934 | 8.4 |
| 1867 | 7.3 | 1901 | 2.7 | | |
| 1868 | 37.3 | 1902 | 5.0 | | |
| 1869 | 73.9 | 1903 | 24.4 | | |
| 1870 | 139.1 | 1904 | 42.0 | | |

marked variation in the pelts of fur-bearing animals, checked over a long term of years, coincides with the Sun-spot cycle; another biological effect of Sun-spot phenomena.

Although the business cycle and the Sun-spot cycle coincide very closely, there have been several lags or discrepancies which science has been unable to satisfy itself on. The factor of planetary refraction seems to have been ignored. Yet if we take cognizance of the planetary revolutions in our solar system and check the varying positions in relation to each other, to the Sun and the Earth, the discrepancies are plain, and explainable by planetary angles and positions.

Apparently then, we cannot use the Sun-spot phenomena alone in forecasting economic probabilities, but include observations of planetary cycles and planetary interaction also. We shall approach this field in the next chapter.

CHAPTER FOUR

# THE PLANETARY CYCLES

Since the ages of antiquity philosophers have viewed the skies. They charted the heavens in relation to a belt or huge circle whose middle line is the ecliptic or Sun's path. The signs of the zodiac are the animal and human forms which seem to be reproduced in the constellations within this belt. During the 4th century the intellectual zodiac was computed. It employs the names of the constellations reckoned from the vernal equinox, each thirty degrees being one sign, irrespective of the relative positions of the corresponding constellations. In these observations we use this intellectual zodiac to observe planetary positions and interaction.

The constellations, through the phenomena of the precession of the equinoxes, gradually slip back through the signs at the rate of 50″ per year, or one whole sign in 2,160 years. The entire revolution of the constellations occupies a period of 25,920 years. At the present time the nodal point of the circle of constellations is leaving the sign Pisces, and, in the next several years, will enter the sign Aquarius. Pisces is indicative of water, religious aspiration, confinement and restraint. The past 2000 years of history marked exploration by water, the development of chemistry, medicine, steam and water power; a new religion gripped the hearts of men that aspired to make man in the image of his god. Intolerance and discipline—a form of restraint—in political, economic and religious thinking was the basis of developing the greatest period of human initiative in known history.

Aquarius is an air sign that typifies aspirations of unity and the establishment of the bond of mutual interests. Its effects are a lack of continuity and stability, but tenacity and decided dependence. The symbol is brotherhood, being mentally dominant in the idea of social interdependence with a dislike of all caste systems in human relationships. Where Pisces is water Aquarius is air and ether; and it follows that the approaching cycle of the Aquarian Age will stress affairs of the air and ether, such as aeronautics; and those things pertaining to light, heat and electronics. At the same time the entire political and social aspects of society will change.

The movements of the planets around the Sun are traced through the zodiac, and computations of their daily positions are published in table form called ephemerides. The time of a complete revolution of a planet around the Sun is termed a planetary year. The earth year is the standard of measurement. The approximate periods of planetary revolutions are:

Earth—365 days 7 hrs.
Mercury—88 days
Venus—224 days
Mars—1 year 322 days
Jupiter—11 yrs 314 days
Saturn—29 yrs 167 days
Uranus—84 years
Neptune—164 yrs 167 days
Moon—28 days around the Earth

Ancient astrology was principally confined to the purposes of divination, or, foretelling specific events by means of a map of the heavens drawn at the moment of broaching the question. In modern times the scientific researcher entirely ignores the practice of interpreting events from these horary figures. Ancient fatalism has become tinctured with free-will, and the modern study of planetary interaction and cosmic vibration is a science that starts where ancient astrology left off.

This new science is thoroughly cognizant with all of the advances and discoveries of modern science. Its development is based on these discoveries. But it fully recognizes the line of demarcation between the fatalism of the Ancients and the doctrine of free-will and ego-centric perspective,—persisted in by current schools of psychology. It is the undiscovered key to psychology, for it shows that man, individually and en masse, is impelled along paths that are definitely related to planetary and other phases of solar radiation.

In checking economic statistics of the business cycle with the periods when the major slow moving planets, Saturn, Uranus and Jupiter, are ninety or one hundred eighty degrees apart in the zodiac, they are found to coincide with economic depression. But when the same planets are sixty or one hundred and twenty degrees apart (in the zodiac) they coincide with periods of prosperity. This phenomena is discussed in detail in a companion brochure.

The earth signs of the zodiac, Taurus, Virgo and Capricorn, have always been closely coupled to American political and financial life. The passage of planets through these signs in their revolutions tie in with major events in a startling manner. For the first time in United States history Jupiter and Saturn began to meet in conjunction in earth signs just after 1840. Regularly every twenty years since a conjunction of these two planets has occurred in these earth signs, timing periods of political upheaval and new agitation, and interest;—in currency, national credit and financial matters.

Every President, since the inception of these conjunctions in earth signs, who was elected in these periods, died in office. In 1840 Harrison was elected and died in office. In 1860 Lincoln was elected. He died in office. Garfield was elected in 1880 and he died in office. In 1900 it was McKinley and in 1920 it was Harding. In 1940 it was Roosevelt; despite increasing disabilities he persisted to re-election in 1944. And in 1960 the sequence continued with Kennedy.*

Wild-cat bank notes, following the panic of 1837–1838, became the "red-dog" variety until agitation for inflation placed all the banks of Michigan in receivership in 1842. In 1861 federal credit was such that non-interest bearing notes were ordered, starting the greenback difficulties. After the veto of the inflationary Bland-Allison Act in 1878 a silver standard was agitated in the depression of 1882 to 1885. Credit problems were so great in 1902–03 panic occurred. After 1920 cheap money and credit was agitated and the Agricultural Act of 1923 resulted.

* This sentence in this 1978 edition brings the cycle to date.

CHAPTER FIVE

# THE URANUS CYCLE

Of the planets comprising the same solar system as the Earth the recently discovered planet Pluto has the largest orbit, taking the longest time to go around the Sun. Neptune is next in order, taking approximately 164 years, 167 days to go around the Sun. The movements of these planets have coincided with epochal changes in the psychology of the people, but just now we are more concerned with the manner in which Uranus has been prominent in American economic history.

Uranus was recognized as being in the heavens in ancient times, but it was not located and astronomically discovered until 1781 by William Herschel. It was first seen in the sign Gemini, and is astrologically attributed to the rulership of Aquarius.

The revolution of Uranus is 84 years, or about seven years in each sign of the zodiac. When at sensitive angles with other planets, or in sensitive points of the zodiac, its effects are sudden and radical changes, secrecy, plotting, estrangements, chaos, and action engendered by an underlying progressiveness. Its general effects generate humanitarian and altruistic endeavors in the positive side, but its negative side generates fanaticism with rather riotous and eccentric activity, disorder and inexplicibly sudden changes of fortune. Its revolutions of 84 years peculiarly align with American history.

The vast researches in history during the past two decades have clarified many heretofore difficult points. Until recently history was viewed principally as a numerical co-ordination of events with the calendar. Now we have come to realize that cycles of history operate in much the same manner as cycles of business, each cycle being an epoch. Many notable studies in the co-ordination and sweep of the cycles of history have been presented in recent years, the "March of Democracy" by James Trueslow Adams, and the "Outline of History" by H. G. Wells being popular examples. The monumental work of Spengler, in "The Decline of the West," even goes a step farther by co-ordinating centuries of human history into a huge connected skein, with each era separated but inter-related with the next.

Few historians, however, have taken any note of the cycles of approximately eighty-four years that have been so closely identified with American life. Whether the newness of Western civilization on the North American continent has prevented the taking of such a major economic perspective of its history, or whether broad perspectives are considered of little value is a debatable affair. At any rate, and in spite of many important intervening events, there have been distinct economic and social cycles of 84 years each. The manner in which these cycles align with the cycles of Uranus has reached a point where it has ceased to be coincidence.

If our historians are correct, Columbus landed on what is now known as the West Indies group of islands in 1492. From 1492 to 1520 Spain gave little attention to the new land except to establish settlements for exploration and trading purposes in the West Indies. The main land was practically ignored. Their search was primarily for gold and treasure, and a new route between Europe and the Far East. Balboa crossed Panama and reached the Pacific in 1513, while Ponce de Leon landed in Florida in the same year. In 1520 Magellan found a strait near the southern end of South America, which settled the question of the position of the America's in relation to Europe and Asia. But it was in the 1520's before any settlement or colonization of the mainland was attempted by white men.

In 1523 and 1524 Florida, the territory which now reaches from Florida to Labrador, attracted the first serious attention of Spain. Late in 1523 the first formal grant of conquest and settlement was issued. The first settlement was launched under d'Ayllon, not far from the same spot on which Jamestown was later founded.

Astronomical calculations indicate that the planet Uranus crossed the 8th and 9th degrees of the zodiacal sign Gemini in the year 1523, coinciding with the first settlement of the land which now comprises part of the United States.

In the 84 years between 1523 and 1607, when Uranus again returned to the 8th and 9th degrees of Gemini, many changes occurred on the North American Continent, but in the light of history this period was a distinct epoch in itself.

Just after the beginning of the 17th century a troublesome depression gripped Europe. Thousands were without employment or even a place to live. The proposal to colonize America met with great favor. Elizabeth was dead. The Stuarts were in the ascendancy and Europe was launching a period of fateful constitutional changes which was sinister and chaotic.

So it was in the latter part of April, 1607, the first English settlement was made in America at Jamestown, Virginia. Notwithstanding the shortcomings of the settlers, their tremendous difficulties and their impracticality in adjusting themselves to a new land, there is no mistaking that this settlement and year was the beginning of the 2nd epoch in American economic history. It also began a new Uranus cycle.

In 1691 Uranus had again traveled through its 84 year orbit, returning again to the 8th and 9th degrees of Gemini. Since 1607 the New England colonies had developed, Maryland was a province and organization had entered Pennsylvania, New Jersey and Carolina. But when the 1690's began civil war and revolution embroiled England, laying the seeds of political and religious dissension in the American colonies. Conditions became so intense in the colonies by 1691 that a general upheaval ensued, which Woodrow Wilson, in his five volume "History of the American people," calls "The Revolution." This deluge ended the 2nd epoch of American economic life which began with the founding of Jamestown in 1607. The 1690's saw the fall and burning of Jamestown, the fall of Plymouth, Massachusetts and Maryland, and the institution of new political currents and economic ideas, coinciding with the beginning of another new cycle of Uranus.

In 1775, 84 years after 1691, Uranus again returned to the 8th and 9th degrees of Gemini. In the interim the seeds of American independence had been sown and on May 20th, 1775, a Declaration of Independence was issued from the Mecklenburg, Virginia Convention. But the new era of independence did not formally begin until Uranus reached 8 degrees 51 minutes of Gemini at 20 minutes past noon on July 4th, 1776 in Philadelphia: when the final Declaration of Independence was signed. Indubitably coinciding with the new cycle of Uranus, the fourth epoch in American economic life began.

Late in 1859, 84 years after the Declaration of Independence, Uranus had again returned to the 8th and 9th degrees of Gemini. In the interim a new union of states developed and multiplied, but, violent dissension had been gaining ground on several major questions ever since the 1820's. By 1850 close to an armed division of affairs developed, which became an actuality in Civil War in 1861. On December 20th, 1860, South Carolina seceded from the union. The planet Uranus was in 9 degrees 17 minutes of Gemini on that day.

On February 4th, 1861 the provisional constitution of the Confederacy was framed at Montgomery, Alabama. Uranus was retrograding in 8 degrees 6 minutes of Gemini at the moment. The first armed conflict of the war took place in early April 1861 at Fort Sumter. Uranus was then in 9 degrees 4 minutes of Gemini.

A reference has already been made to the conjunctions of Jupiter and Saturn beginning to appear in earth signs, after 1840, at approximately 20 year intervals. The conjunction following the presidential election of 1860 occurred on October 21st, 1861 in 18 degrees 22 minutes of Virgo, although between September and November 1861 it was very near a constant conjunction.

At the time of this conjunction period of 1861 the state of federal credit became serious. Tax receipts from the Southern states were no longer sources of income, while the expense of the war was more than the Treasury could stand. In July 1861 only 25 cents of each dollar spent in government came from taxes. The balance was borrowed. Following an appeal to the banks for $150 millions in August the Treasury could not pay creditors in coin and the country went on a paper basis. Between that time and 1863 close to a half billion in greenbacks was issued while gold went to huge premiums. The problem became intensely difficult through the sudden death of Lincoln, when Reconstruction plans and the efforts toward credit stabilization were unexpectedly transferred to Vice President Johnson, a Democrat in what had been a Republican Administration. So without any doubt the crossing of the 8th and 9th degrees of Gemini by Uranus again coincided with the end of one epoch and the beginning of a new fifth epoch in American economic history; intensified by the appearance of the conjunction of Jupiter and Saturn in Virgo.

From 1859–1860 to 1943–1944, when Uranus will again traverse the 8th and 9th degrees of Gemini, is 84 years. Intensifying circumstances at that time will be Saturn in Gemini between May 9th, 1942 and June 20th, 1944, following a conjunction of Saturn and Uranus in 29 degrees of Taurus on May 3rd, 1942, and a conjunction of Jupiter and Saturn in Taurus (an earth sign) in the early part of February 1941. It is unqualifiedly the most momentous period so far encountered in American history.

CHAPTER SIX

# SOME CONCLUSIONS

Any recapitulation of the observations in the foregoing material must first take cognizance of the fact that these cycles are not compelling. If appointed leadership could and would take stock of these phenomena any long range observations could be couched in a pre-adjustment to the reverberations. On the other hand, the very complexities of the headlong welter of public opinion and political expediency seems to bear down as an irremovable force or process of evolution. Preventive prescriptions have no place here, however.

Those practiced in the habit of waiting to see debatable economic effects may conclude that all this data is a unique chain of coincidences which have no bearing on the future. But let us maintain a distinction between that which consists of economic effect and that which may be cause.

The first conclusion is that the period between the World War and the late 1950's marks a cyclical transition from the Piscean Age of the last 2000 years into the Aquarian Age of the next 2000 years. The dead center of the transition computes as the decade of 1940 to 1950.

Second, the fifth 84 year cycle in American economic life will end in 1943 and a new 84 year cycle begin in 1944, a transition heretofore accompanied by tremendous and chaotic circumstances.

Third, a Sun-spot maximum is expected in 1938, and a minimum in 1943 and 1944, which is one contribution to the anticipation that business indices will attain a high in 1938 and a low in 1943 and 1944.

Fourth, a conjunction of Jupiter and Saturn again occurs in an earth sign, this time in 1941, following the election of 1940, suggesting the possibility of a repetition of an unexpected collapse of executive power by 1945.

Fifth, a phenomena of the Jupiter-Saturn conjunctions in earth signs is the manner in which they have timed a new interest in problems of banking, credit and the expansion of credit. When accompanied by Uranian influences, as occurred following 1860, necessitous inflationary expedients developed. Between 1940 and 1945 the combined influences are far more potent than at any time in American history, including the Civil War period. The conclusion is that the aftermath of the credit expansion of the late 1930's will form the beginning of money problems timed for the early 1940's; but, that necessitous and actual inflation will not be probable before 1941 begins. The mass psychology that discounts inflation is of an entirely different order than the fear ridden psychology which accompanies actual inflation. There is a vast difference between actual inflation and credit expansion. The late 1930's appear to mark credit expansion, while the early 1940's point to a necessitous inflationary interval.

The general conclusion is that the business indices will reflect a general upward trend from the lows of 1932 to a high late in 1938. A recession is then expected to begin, with the "normal" downward trend into 1943 and 1944, violently, but only temporarily, interrupted in the inflationary period of 1941 and 1942. After 1943 and 1944 the foundation for major readjustments actually start, so that by 1950 and 1951 another, and greater, epoch in American economic life begins; coinciding with a new 84 year Uranus cycle, plus the 2000 year and long awaited Aquarian Age.

ADDENDA 1978: World War II fades into history but its deep effects have become more and more ominous to the traditions of American life. Standards of value, reduced deficit inflation, traditional morality and confidence in the future have been in erosion. The convenience and miracle of debt credit under the pressures of war seems to have gripped the populace to get a share and elect those who promise it. Inflation is turning from the glow of prosperity to the ogre of deep-seated inflation. This heritage of the 1940's includes the national shift from the concept of independence to that of internationalism which was given birth in the form of the United Nations. After 1950–1951 the promised new epoch did begin even though viewed askance now.

## BIBLIOGRAPHY

*Chapters 2 & 3*

"Principles of Radio Communication" by Morecroft.

"Below Ten Meters" by James Millen and R. S. Kruse.

"Electronics" issue of April 1932.

"Life's Place in the Cosmos" by Hiram Percy Maxim. Appleton 1933.

"Astronomy" by John Charles Duncan, Ph.D. Harpers 1930.

"The Universe Around Us" by James Jeans. MacMillan 1929.

"Earth, Radio and Stars" by Harlan T. Stetson. McGraw-Hill 1934.

"Astro-Economic Research" by L. J. Jensen. Astrological Bulletina Issues 198 & 199.

*Chapter 4*

"Astrological Key Words" by Manly P. Hall. David McKay 1931.

"New Dictionary of Astrology" by Sepharial. David McKay 1928.

"Lilly's Astrology" by William Lilly. G. Bell and Sons Ltd London 1919.

*Chapter 5*

"History of the American People" by Woodrow Wilson. Five vols. Harpers 1901 1902.

"Florida—Old and New" by Dau. Putnam's 1934.

"Romantic and Historic Florida" by A. Hyatt Verrill. Dodd, Mead 1935.

"Roger Williams" by James E. Ernst. MacMillan 1932.

"A Century of Banking Progress" by Wm. O. Scroggs, Ph.D. Doubleday, Page 1924.

# Section II

# ASTRO-ECONOMIC INTERPRETATION

## A MUNDANE ASTROLOGY NOTEBOOK

### FUNDAMENTALS OF ECONOMIC FORECASTING



(**NOTE**: Chapters 1 to 8 inclusive; material to follow is all new for this edition.)

# FOREWORD

The scientific world has come far since that day when the French Academy of Science examined Edison's first phonograph and pronounced it a clever hoax and product of ventriloquism. But as great as the mechanical and electrical advances have been, it is only recently that more than desultory attention has been paid to astrological premises. The average individual fears that which he does not understand. The air of mystery surrounding astrology simply accentuates this intellectual fear. The normal "protective" reaction is then derision, and sometimes, castigation. Until recently this "protective" derision toward astro-science tenets has persisted with almost fanatical zeal. Now, however—for with knowledge develops understanding—serious consideration involves the subject.

The enormous findings and progress in radio and electronics, aerodynamics, weather cycles, et cetera, during recent years, has aroused a new interest in the related astrological premises which have been the common knowledge of researchers since the days of the Chaldeans and Egyptians. It is part of our rapidly moving epoch that much of this ancient material be correlated and clarified so that the modern layman can both approach and understand the field.

This manual makes no pretense of being either an encyclopedia, a complete compendium, or even an introductory dictionary of astrological tenets and practice. Such a work would include a great deal of the philosophical and scientific works of history, plus dozens of volumes of observation in astrological material. This work is, however, the outgrowth of a need for a ready reference book which would afford the salient working or everyday basis for interpreting Cosmic forces from ephemerides. It is the result of innumerable methods of procedure that were carefully tested in over fifteen years of observation and study. Several methods not included herein, though quite widely used, must be rejected for both unscientific and practical test reasons. However, fifteen years of intensive research is far too short a time in which to formulate even one dogmatic postulate on the invalidity of any method in this gigantic field of observation. We are barely on the threshold of astrological application to economic, political, social and individual maladjustments with natural laws and forces. The material herein is therefore a foundation for practical procedure.

Although general economics long since applied detailed observational concentration to mass psychology, nationalities, and group movements; and then formulated individual reactions through group stimuli, environmental contacts, and heredity, to the potentialities and possibilities of one person, astrology has blandly given little attention to anything but the individual. This cart before the horse procedure has obviously retarded any general understanding of the subject, and, at the same time, prevented an intensive and organized research into its principles. When a business organization prepares to open a new territory they carefully survey the new field for not only the possible demand for their goods, but whether large numbers of the population are sufficiently prosperous to buy. If the territory is generally prosperous then the average inhabitant is prosperous.

The detailed attention to natal astrology, or the analysis of the individual, has tended researchers to overlook the extreme importance in a geographical location and its astrological portents. It is banal to suggest a field for electrical refrigerators north of the Arctic Circle, yet it is almost as trivial to insist that the individual is not governed by the group and location where he lives. Therefore Mundane or National Astro-Analysis is the first and most important part of astrological interpretation. Without it distinct progress in natal astrology would continue to remain scientifically fragmentary.

In spite of the importance of the mundane field there are only a handful of three or four published works on the subject, although the materials on personal genitures run into hundreds of volumes. This is probably a normal sequence to every individuals' love of self being first in his or her thinking. Each person is interested in his tendencies, his destiny, his opportunities, and his chances for finding mental co-ordination and happiness. Yet in these days when the world is attempting to cast off the remnants of a Stone Age individualism in preparation for the New Age of co-operation, it is realized that the Not-Self—the circumstances around us—is of greater importance than the Self—our own personal ego. So it is that the mundane field of astrology is both the key to national events and individual attainment.

This brief brochure attempts to present thoroughly tested and practical methods of procedure correlated into as simplified formulae as the present state of the art permits. No new theories or startling departures from recognized fundamentals are suggested, even though many of the currently popular theories have been tested and so far found wanting in results. The layman whose astrological experience has been confined to a few Sun-Sign readings and a perusal of a few magazines is invited to carefuly study the recent brochure, "Major Trends in American Economics," in order to grasp the fundamentals involved in interpretive work.

I am gratefully indebted to a vast number of authors and correspondents throughout the world in aligning the procedure herein. The interchange and sifting of the multitude of ideas and premises received through these contacts has been of inestimable value. Probably the only original feature of the entire work lies in the correlation of the methods of procedure. Credit could well be given to a list of researchers and authors too numerous to append. However, I am particularly grateful to Mr. George J. McCormack, not only as a fellow researcher in the American Academy of Astrologians, and the voluminous mass of data we have discussed in the last several years, but for a part of the radix figure material which forms such a vital part of the data included herein.

It is mildly probable that this material may come to the attention of others than researchers quite conversant with astrological procedure, practice and fundamentals. To these, it should be reminded, that astrological interpretation is an art rather than an exact science. It deals with the entire pattern of human life, from world economics and religion to every detail of individual life. Expect far more from the subject than has yet been attained by the combined efforts of governments, politics, industry and finance in heavily subsidized natural phenomena research, but don't expect the impossible. Medical science is still fifty per cent guess work, the administration of governments continues to be principally dependent on political emotion, while orthodox economics has made slight progress in coping with the maladjustments of human life. Astro-science has a far better record to offer, in spite of the situation that research into its scientific postulates is yet in its infancy, but allow for some interpretive error.

KANSAS CITY, NOVEMBER 1935 L. J. JENSEN

CHAPTER ONE

# MUNDANE RULERSHIPS

Tradition teaches that the signs of the zodiac, the symbols of planets and the earthly influences of both, were a heavenly revelation to man from the dark ages of the past. Since the time of the Chaldeans the fundamental traditions of astrological practice have persisted unchanged. However, since the tremendous strides in astronomy, electrical applications, and aeronautics, in the last half a century, a new depth of understanding has become applied to the ancient premises of stellar science. Accordingly, a new foundation for mundane astrology interpretation is developing.

Mundane astrology is the study of cosmic forces in relation to the activity, events and circumstances of countries, cities and groups of people. It is astrological economics; or, astro-economics, for purposes of brevity.

The major problem in astro-economics has been the allocation of zodiacal and planetary rulerships so as to co-ordinate the positions of the astral bodies with a specific latitude and longitude on the earth's surface. A number of earnest researchers have developed several methods of co-ordination, but a complete simplified synthesis has never been offered. The work of Johndro in "The Earth in the Heavens," Counsil in the "Cyclic Locality Dial" and "X Marks My Place," and Sepharial in the "Theory of Geodectic Equivalents" bear both the necessity for careful examination and profound respect. The thesis developed does much to clarify the entire problem.

However, the problem does not end with sign rulerships. It includes a difficulty with the two-sign rulerships of Mercury, Venus and Mars that are one of the problems handed down from antiquity. These two elements of the rulership problem have probably been the greatest deterrents to astro-economic interpretation progress.

The people of the present civilization appear to be members of a Fifth Race that have inhabited the earth. The divisions of the Zodiac as viewed by this Race locates the sign Leo in the fifth segment of the Zodiac. Leo, the fifth sign, is ruled by the Sun. And the Sun is the center of the planetary system of which the earth is a part. The other planets are attributed to govern, or rule, the signs following the sign Leo in the order of their distance from the Sun, viz, Mercury rules Virgo, Venus Libra, Mars Scorpio, Jupiter Sagittarius, Saturn Capricorn, Uranus Aquarius, and Neptune Pisces.

Until recently the rulerships ended there, although the Moon has always been attributed to Cancer in modern times, while Aries suggested Mars, Venus Taurus, and Gemini Mercury. However, in my own practice there have been repeated circumstances which indicated that more than Mars, Venus, Mercury, and the Moon involved Aries, Taurus, Gemini and Cancer.

In 1930 the planet called Pluto was located. Its revolution around the

Sun is computed as about 330 years. Therefore, if the continuity of rulerships applies, Pluto logically takes its place as the planetary ruler of the sign Aries. Then during the course of time three more planets, to assume rulerships of Taurus, Gemini and Cancer, will be located. As Pluto has two times the revolution of Neptune and Neptune is about twice the time in revolution as Uranus the next planetary discovery will probably have a revolution period of about 660 years, and so on. When the planet ruling Cancer is discovered the rulership of the Moon will then revert to Pars Fortuna.

In assigning sign rulerships care is necessary in attributing too much certainty that Mars completely rules Aries, or Venus Taurus, Mercury Gemini and the Moon Cancer. They do partially rule these divisions, but apparently only as lower (more physical) octaves of the principal ruling planets which have not yet been astronomically located. In interpretation we shall continue to attribute Mars to Aries though it is subordinate to Pluto as the full ruler. In other words Mars is full ruler over Scorpio but simply a partial and lower octave ruler of Aries, Venus rules Libra but is only a partial or lower octave ruler of Taurus, and so on with Mercury and Gemini and the Moon and Cancer. The resulting balance is graphically illustrated in a diagram in the note section.

But the problem of aligning zodiacal positions with latitude and longitude on the earth is more difficult to most observers. Literally a multitude of attempts have been published on the subject, some involving a heliocentric bases, others a precessional geocentric, and others simply philosophical conjecture. All of them have a basis in fact, depending on a particular approach, yet none of them have worked consistently for me. After a great deal of effort, however, the problem appears solved as so far repeated tests have brought consistently satisfactory results. Lengthy discussion has no place here, but each point is amply explained by Alan Leo in his "Casting the Horoscope" although he seems to miss the application.

In the 1917 Yearbook of the American Academy of Astrologians Florence Adele Barnett applied the zodiacal signs to longitude along the Equator and placed 0° of Taurus at the longitude of the Pyramid of Gizeh. The signs of the zodiac were measured EAST in their regular order. The Pyramid is located at 31° 07½′ East Longitude. Voluminous researches in connection with Pyramid measurements clearly prove the scientific basis for this co-ordination. Some of these items are available in "A Miracle in Stone" by Joseph A. Seiss, D. D. although it presents only a small part of the material. The signs are located as follows:

| | | | | | | |
|---|---|---|---|---|---|---|
| 0° Aries - | 1° 07 ½′ | EAST | Long. | 0° Libra - | 178° 52 ½′ | WEST |
| 0° Taurus | 31° 07 ½′ | " | " | 0° Scorpio | 148° 52 ½′ | " |
| 0° Gemini | 61° 07 ½′ | " | " | 0° Sagittarius | 118° 52 ½′ | " |
| 0° Cancer | 91° 07 ½′ | " | " | 0° Capricorn | 88° 52 ½′ | " |
| 0° Leo | 121° 07 ½′ | " | " | 0° Aquarius | 58° 52 ½′ | " |
| 0° Virgo | 151° 07 ½′ | " | " | 0° Pisces | 28° 52 ½′ | " |

From ancient times it has been recognized that the Zodiac is a fixed belt formed by the *earth's orbit around the Sun.* It has none of the irregularity of the constellations and it is the actual zodiac of geocentric computations. It has no relation to the Zodiac of the Constellations; when we are thinking in terms of the Universe in relation to the precession of the equinoxes which at some, at present, astronomically unknown period left 0° of Aries and now lies somewhere between 28° of Aries and 8° to 10° of Pisces. The actual and geocentric zodiac is as fixed today as it was several thousands of years ago. The modern geocentric ephemeris does not revise the heliocentric positions to align with the mythical 0° Aries of the Zodiac of the Constellations; it simply gives the positions of the planets geocentrically instead of heliocentrically. The actual zodiac used in interpretation is right in step with equinoxtial precession and always has been. Therefore each country and city has the same rulership as it always has had; but, when we go outside of our solar system to compute fixed star effects we step into the Zodiac of the Constellations which is a matter of precession. Therefore we can go further in aligning rulerships mundanly.

During a period of ten years I traveled almost continuously, crossing and recrossing forty-six states of the United States and four Canadian provinces. In that time repeated observation was made of the probable ruling degrees of cities and towns. Every type of constellation coordinate was used but the varying success could only be attributed to Ascendants and not the mid-heaven points. Yet the Pyramid co-ordination worked consistently and faithfully. Another suggestion of Miss Barnett's was, that in accordance with the mystical revelation number 144, or 12 times 12, each of the twelve signs be divided into twelve subdivisions of 2½°, and that as Taurus is aligned with the Pyramid location the first 2½° sub-division of each sign be allotted to Taurus instead of Aries. But this did not work in practice and its only scientific basis lay in a rather distant occult point.

In some of the Hindu material forwarded me by H. M. Poojara in Kathiawar, India, were notes on some of the esoteric phases of the Dwadasamsas, or 2½° divisions of the Hindu zodiac. (See the frontispiece of Alan Leo's "Esoteric Astrology" for this chart). According to this method of sub-division, and there are many occult and scientific reasons involved, the first Dwadasamsas of each sign is held by the same sign; the first sub-division of Aries is Aries, but the first subdivision of Taurus is not Aries but is Taurus. Two charts, one showing the major zodiacal divisions of the world and the other the major and sub-divisions for the United States, are on the pages following. Suffice it to say that this co-ordination works; always.

To compute the major division mid-heaven degree for any location add 1° 7½′ to WEST Longitude and divide the total by 30° (one sign). The amount over, in degrees, subtract from 30°. The first gives the number of signs (counting BACKWARDS from the usual order) and the second is the degree of rulership on the M. C. of the location. In the Table of Houses locate this M. C. degree in the proper latitude column and then enter cuspal positions on the chart. To illustrate:

| Kansas City, Mo. — | West Longitude | 94° 30′ |
|---|---|---|
| | ADD | 1° 7½′ |
| | | 95° 27½′ |

Dividing by 30°gives 3 signs 5° 37½

Subtracting the result from 30° gives 24° 32½′

So, the zodiacal position of the M. C. is Sagittarius 24° 32½′
The Latitude is 39° North. In the Table of Houses 24° Sagittarius on the M. C. is 19° 4′ Pisces on the Ascendant.

To compute the sub-division rulership; each sub-division is 2½° so 24° is in the 10th Dwadasamsas, which, under Sagittarius is Virgo. The beginning of this 10th Dwadasamsas is 7½° from 0° Capricorn at 88° 52½′ West Longitude at 96° 22½′ West. Kansas City is 24° 32½′ Sagittarius (94° 30′ West); a difference of 112½′. As one thirtieth of 2½° is 5′ then 112½′ computes to 22 degrees of Virgo which is the sub-division MC bringing an ascendant of 6° 06′ of Sagittarius at 39 North Latitude. By using your slide rule the computations are greatly simplified.

A few of the major division degrees are as follows:

| | | | | |
|---|---|---|---|---|
| Boston | 18° Capricorn | on M. C. | 4° Taurus | on Asc. |
| New York | 15° Capricorn | " " | 28° Aries | " " |
| Washington | 12° Capricorn | " " | 22° Aries | " " |
| Chicago | 2° Capricorn | " " | 4° Aries | " " |
| Los Angeles | 1° Sagittarius | " " | 15° Aquarius | " " |

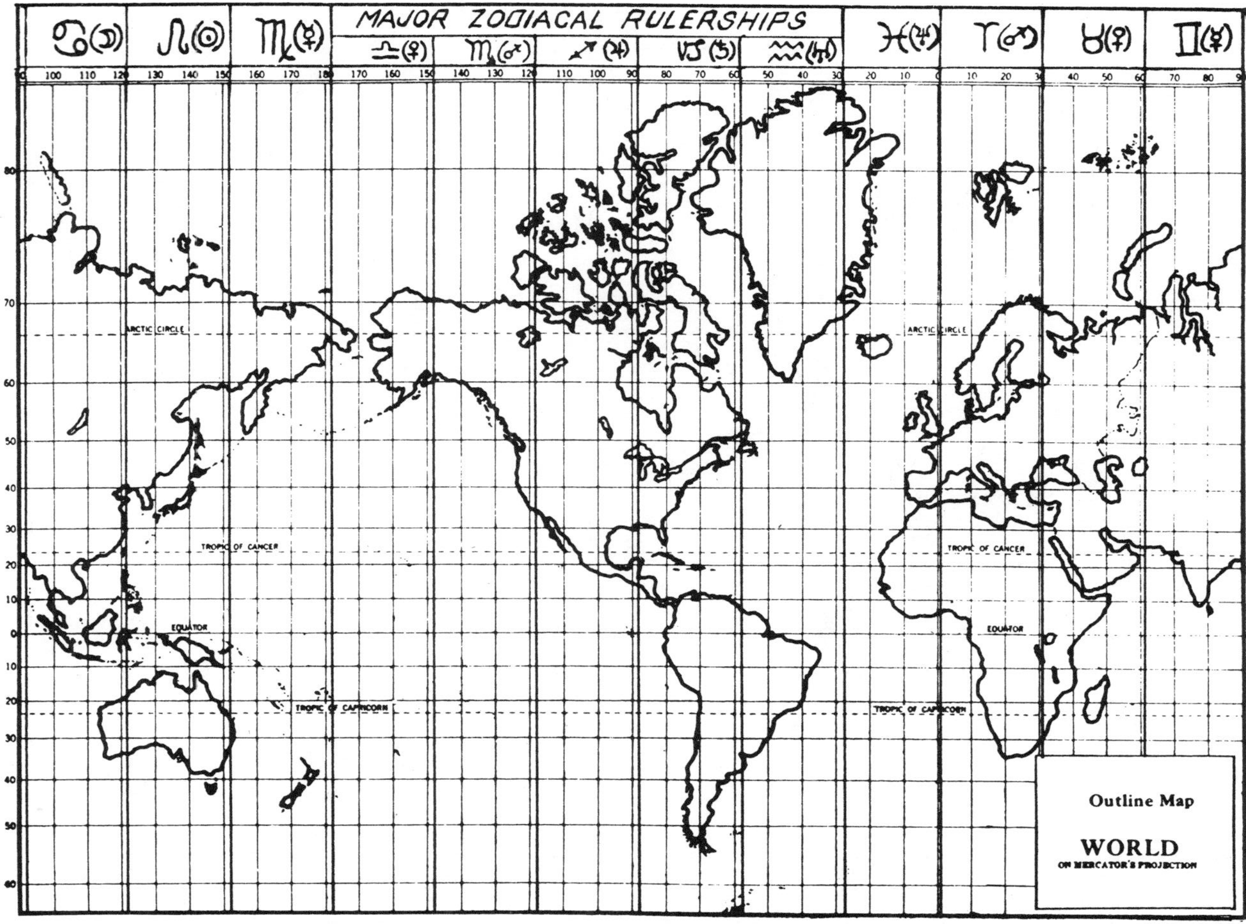
MAJOR ZODIACAL RULERSHIPS
ARCTIC CIRCLE
TROPIC OF CANCER
EQUATOR
TROPIC OF CAPRICORN
Outline Map
WORLD
ON MERCATOR'S PROJECTION

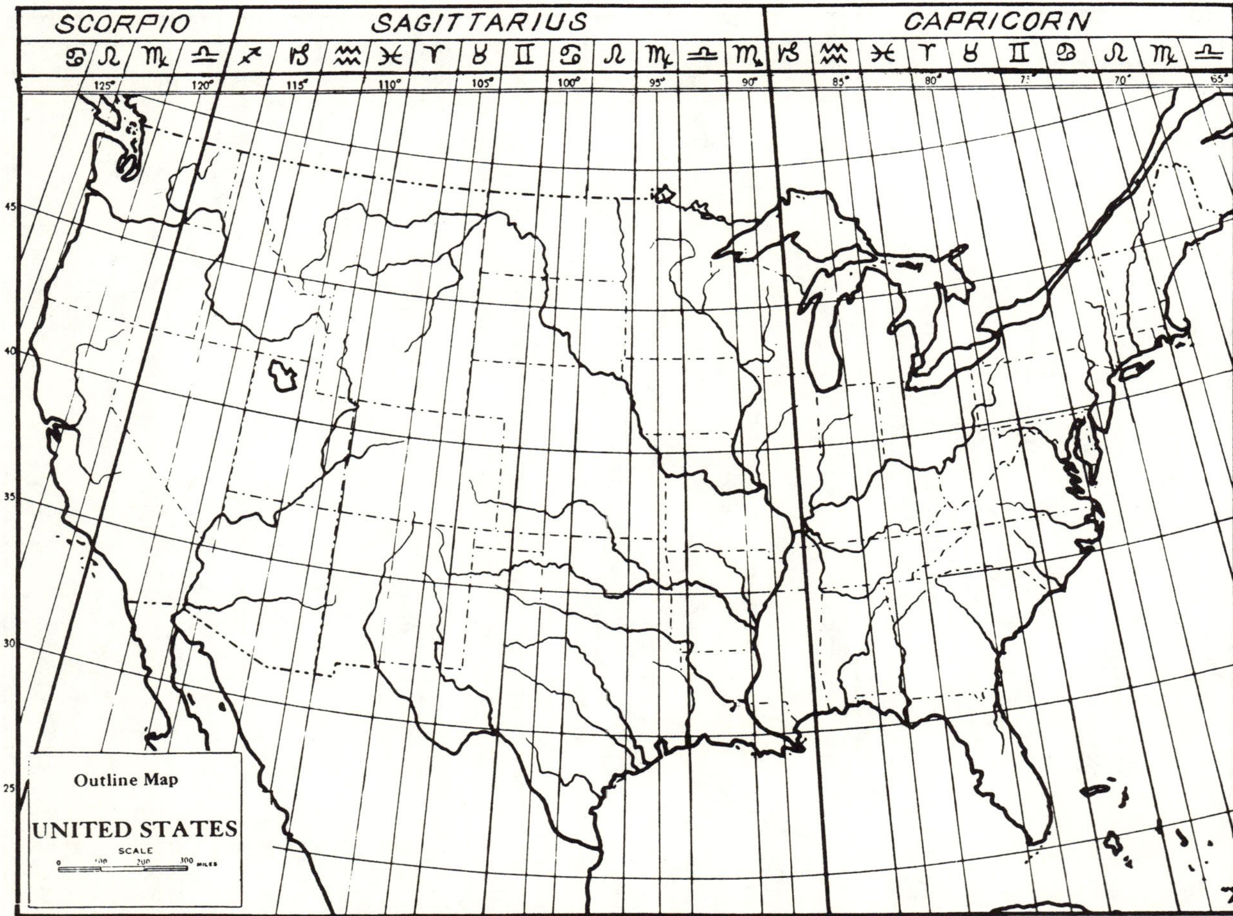

SCORPIO
SAGITTARIUS
CAPRICORN
Outline Map
UNITED STATES
SCALE
0 100 200 300 MILES
Longitude West of Greenwich

CHAPTER TWO

# PROGRESSIONS AND TRANSITS

One of the most difficult problems in astrological practice is the method to use in projecting or "progressing" a radix or birth chart in order to analyze the probabilities of the future. The controversies on this point are very heated, and tend to diffuse most of the fundamentals involved. The many facets of the question have no place in a note-book manual of this sort, but I have found that every method in general use has some basis of merit. On the other hand, a small degree of merit is unsatisfactory excuse for using methods which do not stand up consistently. In mundane interpretation results are of paramount importance.

The popular methods of "primary" and "secondary" directions have never held up for me. In other words, they work beautifully one time and fail utterly at another. Mentally leaping the gap by presuming transit "touch-offs" or changes in geographical location never explained the problem. The obvious answer should be that planetary positions on the tenth or twentieth days after the beginning or birth cannot have any effect on the corresponding years of life. It is physically impossible to raise a blister in the twentieth year because of a burn received on the twentieth day. Yet, like the progressive motion of the precession of the equinoxes, and the entire Solar system, there is an analogy between a day and a year in interpretive science. It is the occult, the fatalistic, and also probably the expression of the microcosmic within the macrocosmic. The diurnal cycle is related to the annual cycle in the same manner as the spiritual is related to the physical. One day does relate to one year. But, and this seems to be the point, the diurnal and annual (apparent) revolutions of the Sun are the units of measure; not the zodiacal measures of Mercury, or Mars, or Venus, et cetera. The zodiacal position of Mercury twenty days after birth is effective twenty days after birth but never affects the twentieth year of life. Yet the diurnal, or Sun, measure for the twentieth day of life affects the twentieth year as spiritual, or fatalistic, indicator of the destiny.

The Sun in its diurnal revolution then becomes the basis of progression in locating the destiny of the radix subject. It is the key which reveals why everyone, in a true sense, is neither "captain of his soul or master of his fate." It reveals the Radix subject's relation to inscrutable and imponderable spiritual law.

Sepharial in "The Science of Foreknowledge," Alec Stuart in "The Secret of the Meridian" and particularly Vivian E. Robson in "The Radix System" apply this premise in a most practical and workable manner. When the diurnal measure of the Sun (about 59′ 8″) is applied in each progressed year to every planet in the radix the unit of the solar measurement fulfills the entire analogy of the basic premise involved. The point is that it works out most satisfactorily in practice, without the gaps of the "primary" and "secondary" methods.

ADDENDA 1977: Since the foregoing, written in 1936, the radix system concept has been widely researched in Europe and brilliantly presented in several books by REINHOLD EBERTIN of Aalen, West Germany Significant are "Combination of Stellar Influences," "Tables of Events," "Transits," etc.

For precise work, and where the ephemeris of the radix year is available, the procedure is to take the position of the Sun at the day of the Radix in the ephemeris. Count forward as many days as years are to be progressed and compute exactly how many degrees, minutes and seconds the Sun moved. Add this amount to the longitude of every planet in the Radix and also to all cusp positions. "Secondary" directions occur when the Moon's total travel is added to the position of the Moon in the Radix.

When the ephemeris of the year of the Radix is not available use the average daily rate of the Sun's travel—59′ 8″ for each year; and the average daily travel of the Moon—13° 10′ 35″, for the "secondary" directions. The condensed table of measure will be found in the note section. This method is valuable in estimating the "fate" or long term outlook from corporation, national and other mundane figures. The portents do not involve specific happenings however. Always keep in mind that they simply time the indications or materialization of the indications of the Radix.

For practical and detailed interpretation and forecasts of specific tendencies and events an application of the annual revolution of the Sun seems consistently accurate. The basis is the annual return of the Sun to the same position it occupies in the Radix. A chart set for this moment indicates the events of the year to follow, and diurnal figures based on this Solar Return times those events and indicates by daily and actual planetary positions in operation the motivation and specific timing of all events.

The method is to erect a chart for the moment of the Sun's return to the position it occupied in the Radix. Then the Sidereal Time of this chart is a base for each diurnal chart of the year. For practical purposes one minute (1′) of Sidereal Time is added to the Radix Sidereal Time for each day after the day of the Solar Return, and the ephemeris positions of the planets are the diurnal day in question are entered in their proper places. For example:

Compute the Sun's exact position in the Radix. Then erect a figure for the nearest previous Solar Return to that place. It will be necessary to compute the time of the Return to minutes and seconds in Greenwich Mean Time. Then transpose this G. M. T. to True Local Time by subtracting four minutes for each degree of WEST Longitude, or ADDING four minutes for each degree of EAST Longitude. Then calculate the Sidereal Time of the Solar Return at the geographical location in question, which may not be the Radix location. This Sidereal Time is the base for the diurnal figures of the year, by simply adding one minute for each day to the Solar Return S. T. For illustration, say the Sidereal Time of the Solar Return figure is 12–24–31, September 1st. We want the diurnal for November 1st. To the Sidereal Time of the September

1st chart add one minute (1′) for each day, (30 days from September 1st to October 1st; 31 days from October 1st to November 1st) or 61′.

| | | | |
|---|---|---|---|
| 12 | 24 | 31 | S. T. Solar Return (Sept. 1st) |
| | 61 | | Increase |
| 13 | 25 | 31 | S. T. of Diurnal (Nov. 1st) |

Enter the house cusps according to the proper latitude and the planets positions from the ephemeris for November 1st. The Radix and progressed Radix positions are added in their proper sign positions.

The theory involving this method is that although the sidereal year and the tropical year only differ by the amount of the precession of the equinox (about 50″.2), the sidereal year is 365.25636 mean solar days while there is a sidereal time difference of about six hours, or one quarter day, between two Solar Returns. Our calendar handles this by computing one year as 365 days and every fourth year adding a day. To illustrate: Use the Sun's return at 0° Aries in a geocentric ephemeris.

| *Solar Return* | *Greenwich Time* |
|---|---|
| March 21st, 1929 | 2:35 A.M. |
| March 21st, 1930 | 8:30 A.M. |
| March 21st, 1931 | 2:06 P.M. |
| March 20th, 1932 | 7:54 P.M. (Leap Year) |
| March 21st, 1933 | 1:43 A.M. |
| March 21st, 1934 | 7:28 A.M. |
| March 21st, 1935 | 1:18 P.M. |
| March 20th, 1936 | 6:58 P.M. (Leap Year) |

Twenty four hours of mean solar time are equal to 24 hours, 3 minutes, and 56.5554 seconds of sidereal time. This, however, at the rate of gain of 3 minutes, 56½ minutes a day approximates an entire day each year and so prevents any upset to our premise.

For strictly precise work in the diurnal charts it would have to be recognized that the orbital speed of the Earth around the Sun is not uniform, but varies in accordance with Kepler's principle of the Law of Areas. There is an equation of time in the difference between mean and apparent solar, or Sun, time. This reaches as great a maximum value as PLUS 14 minutes 28 seconds on February 11th, and as much as MINUS 16 minutes 21 seconds on November 3rd. Therefore the Sidereal Time difference between two Solar Returns, computed at 0° of Aries, will be between five and one half and six hours;—not exactly one quarter day each year. To compute the exact daily increment of Sidereal Time to be added to diurnal charts it would be necessary to locate the daily orbital speed of the Earth; or else, divide the total sidereal time differential, between the two Solar Returns involved, by 365.25. But in interpretation we are not concerned with exact aspects, inasmuch as there is an orb of influence in all planetary vibrations. This greatly simplifies matters as for all general purposes we can simply add one minute (1′) for a day.

In interpretation of these diurnal charts, house rulerships, as outlined in the note section, and cuspal points, should receive greatest attention.

A complete pattern of the actual cosmic stimuli, as it is applying at the specific geographical location in question, is patterned on the chart. Events cannot only be timed to the hour but often to the minute. When used with the United States charts the coincidence with governmental acts, news events, and important decisions is often astonishing. The application is more fully discussed in the section on Synthesis.

ADDENDA 1978: readers of the foregoing material in the 1936 edition reproduced here complained of computation problems. Short-cut or more simplified methods were requested. I admit the subsequent demands of daily work forced faster although less precise mathematics, with good quality results. See the chapter: An "Over"-Simplified Method, etc.

CHAPTER THREE

# SYNTHESIS—ESTIMATING ECONOMIC TRENDS

In spite of the many mechanical problems involved in astro-science, the greater difficulty concerns interpretation of the charts. The approach toward precise interpretation can be taught, but the actual interpretation must be learned. No one can teach the actual synthesis of all the potentialities of a chart; it is a natural ability of co-ordination one either possesses or is without. However, there are many salient factors which anyone, with some application and study, can apply and use for practical purposes. If these factors are applied properly the layman is able to attain results quicker, while the practiced interpreter can achieve better results.

Planets are in constant angular relationship to one another and to the earth. Each angle is a different facet or blend of the vibratory forces involved and results in a different psychological motivation than another angle. Every degree of 360° has its specific nature. For practical purposes, and in line with the rules involving angles graphically illustrated and discussed in the companion brochure "Market Charts," only a few of the angles can be considered. These angles, or aspects, principally used are the 30°, 60°, 90°, 120°, 150° and 180° on both sides of the circle. Sometimes the angles of 45° and 135° are also valuable indicators. None of these aspects are, in a true sense, unfavorable; but, as some generate compression while others generate expansion, the tendency is to term the compression aspects unfavorable and the expansion aspects favorable. The 30°, 60°, and 120° are favorable; the 150° is doubtful, and the remainder unfavorable.

In the synthesis of a chart the natures of the planets, the personality of each sign, the meanings of the houses and a knowledge of the aspects are all involved. The chart is like a jar of fluid arriving in the laboratory for analysis. The chemist analyzes the fluid for its complete content. The interpreter of a chart proceeds in the same manner, weighing each part.

In estimating business and market trends my first procedure is to locate the primary, or major, swings of the indices involved. This appears to be involved in the Great Mutation of 240 years portent. Set a Solar Return figure based on this radix (see note section for chart) each year. For the day to day indications use the diurnal method already discussed. The radix and the diurnals are set for the capital of the country in question.

Such a series of charts set over the last seventy five years show a coincidence between the unfavorable aspects of major planets and economic depression, and the favorable aspects with recovery and prosperity. In this period the thirteen times Uranus and Saturn were in unfavorable aspect coincides with thirteen periods of general economic decline. In the nine times these planets were in favorable aspect decided gains in business activity were registered seven times, and mild gains in two times. Since 1896 Uranus and Jupiter have been in favorable aspect twenty eight times. In every case these aspects coincided with gains in business activity. The July 8th, 1932 depression low coincided with an exact trine of these planets on July 9th, 1932—the day the upward thrust began. A synthesis of the relationships by aspect and sign positions of Jupiter, Saturn and Uranus, plus the Sun Spot Cycle is the framework upon which to project the primary trends of business and markets. Additional details are brought out in the companion brochure, "Major Trends in American Economics."

To discover how the national cycles of business, or the primary trends, will effect a particular locality superimpose the Solar Return and diurnals on the house positions of the locality in question according to the rulership procedure in Chapter One.

The intermediate, or secondary, trends within the primary trend become more involved. The primary trend base is retained in mind as of major importance; then a figure is set for the Vernal Equinox. This figure holds rule for the year and the diurnals for each day to follow are based on its Sidereal Time. However, the implications of the quarterly Ingresses which follow take precedence over the particular quarter involved.

The minor trends, seldom of more than a few days duration in the same direction on the statistical charts of business activity and markets, are the most difficult procedure of the three types of trends included. In normal times, where supply and demand operates freely, a barrage or string of favorable aspects will bring upward movements, and a string of unfavorable aspects the reverse. But when periods of abnormality occur, and the economic machinery is broken down, the rule of favorable and unfavorable aspects does not hold *on the minor trend* because of one or more major motivating forces which cuts off or neutralizes the temporary minor forces. Such situations develop regularly, such as the opposition aspect of Saturn to Neptune which was in force during 1935 and will be more strongly in force in the first ten months of 1936. Lunation figures reveal their influences.

The change from one sign to another by a planet coincides with change in trend and general psychology, depending on the magnitude and speed of the planet. Mercury changing signs is a powerful market factor, for instance, in this connection.

In commodity markets the Moon is important in marking turns. The time of the New Moon, or Lunation, and the Full Moon, are critical commodity points; and, if a commodity makes a high (or a low) on one key day it will maintain its new trend until the next key day. Occasionally key days develop simultaneously and thereby mark extremely critical points. Those days termed key days are when the Moon is in square aspect to either Mercury, Mars or Venus. Another factor of importance, particularly in commodity markets, are the planetary hours of each day. Their use in hour to hour observations is of great value.

For corporation events, and the probable activity of their securities, use as a radix chart the mundane house positions described in Chapter One; and the methods of Chapter Two set for the date of incorporation and located at the place of the home office. If the exact data is known set the diurnals according to the Sidereal Time of the exact Solar Return. If not, it is best to watch the interaction of the transits in connection with the incorporation radix set for the home office location and its radix positions and progressions, according to mundane rulership cusps.

Some success can be attained by using the diurnals based on the Solar Return of the New York Stock Exchange radix *at the corporation home office location* and superimposing the corporation radix positions on the diurnals. In the matter of markets, however, it must be stressed that technical market factors, and particularly the statistical market charts, are the yardsticks of market action. Motivating influences are reflected by the planetary positions, but there must be a yardstick first.

The student of business trends quickly realizes that it is a fundamental law that supply and demand are never equal for any length of time. All the man made economic planning ever conceived will never upset that law. The problem of droughts, insects, scourges and rainfall can never be completely controlled in growing commodities. An average of many crops will about coordinate with basic demand, but to have every crop at exactly the average is impossible. Yet shortages at one geographical location and surpluses at another can be detected by the interweaving cycles which average out to the major cycle. These interweaving cycles can be estimated for mundane rulerships (geographical locations) by using major conjunctions as the radix or beginning point. The rotational conjunctions are very useful also.

In the Jupiter-Saturn Rotational Radix (see chart section) the point of wheat is found by subtracting the position of the Sun (at the conjunction moment) from the position of the conjunction and adding the Ascendant. This is a radix point entered and used in much the same manner as Pars Fortuna is used in a natal chart. In the 1901 figure for London this point fell in the second house in conjunction with the Moon at 12° 36′ Cancer and opposing the point of conjunction at 14° 0′ 18″ Capricorn. This figure included the period of the War, when wheat shortages were intense. In the 1921 Conjunction (Jupiter-Saturn) at London the point of wheat is in 10° 43′ Leo in conjunction with Neptune and Venus. The point of barley is found by subtracting the place of the Moon from the place of Jupiter and adding the ascendant; sugar by subtracting Mercury from Venus and adding ascendant; rye by subtracting Mercury from Saturn and adding ascendant; cotton by subtracting Mercury from Mars and adding ascendant. These "points" are to use for supplemental purposes, however, for though they work in a unique manner the scientific basis for them is not clear. The basic idea was suggested by Pallicus in an unpublished manuscript now in the British Museum.

The cycles of each planet, viz, Mars, Venus, etc, are so well known as significant co-ordinates with the cycles of various phases of economic life that they need not be repeated here except to call attention to them. The layman will find the seven lessons on Mundane Astrology, issued by the Brotherhood of Light at Los Angeles, valuable in this connection.

In the problems involving aspects, orbs of influence, etc, the probable moment of greatest intensity of an aspect is sometimes disconcerting. At one time, particularly where mundane rulership figures are concerned and in aspects to cusps and radix positions in diurnal figures, aspects seem to be strongest when approaching than when exact or passing. At other moments the reverse seems to occur. It is not the fault of the computations in the ephemeris or the figure involved, but appears to be caused by the mean obliquity of the Ecliptic. In 1936 this is 23° 26′ 51″.40; the difference between the earth's poles and the ecliptic's poles. This obviously throws every point of the zodiac measured at the Equator, except Aries and Libra degrees, off in declination from one to four degrees. Depending on the declination depends whether the approaching, the exact, or the passed aspect is most powerful. Such a situation can delay a market turn, marked by an aspect of slow moving planets, as much as several months; and in the case of an aspect of rapidly moving planets, several days (and of course, conversely, *ahead* of the ephemeral positions). This is particularly noticeable in 1935 when the important aspects involving Gemini, Cancer and Leo practically all were strongest when approaching or ahead of time, while those involving Sagittarius and Capricorn were behind time. This is a problem to involve careful consideration by observers.

CHAPTER FOUR

# THE HOUSES IN MUNDANE AND CORPORATION CHARTS

*FIRST HOUSE:* General circumstances and temper of the people, their general health and vitality and sense of optimism or pessimism.

CORPORATION: The place of the corporation in relation to the public, its stockholders, and business objectives. (Note ruler of asc. and aspects).

*SECOND HOUSE:* Government Treasury, banking and currency conditions, business and trade activity, taxation and national income; all matters of money.

CORPORATION: earnings and profit abilities.

*THIRD HOUSE:* Transportation and communications, including rails, telephone and telegraph, commercial radio, demand for stocks and bonds, trade volume, technical publications, financial and trade relations with adjacent countries, short distance travel.

CORPORATION: Relations with competitors, transportation and communications, some advertising, bookkeeping accounts, internal agreements.

*FOURTH HOUSE:* Real property, mining, crops, public works and buildings, weather, anti-administration faction in politics, exploration, socialization.

CORPORATION: Tangible assets, direct competition, power of competitors, hazards involving property.

*FIFTH HOUSE:* Amusements and entertainment, including theatres and radio; phases of publishing, publicity and advertising; children and places where women and children congregate; the emotional aspects of mass psychology; domestic welfare of the nation; speculative activity and conditions.

CORPORATION: Subsidiaries or branches, advertising success, income from capital, the place of deposit of capital such as safes, vaults, and banks, the motivating center.

*SIXTH HOUSE:* The state of public health, Army and Navy, condition of the masses—particularly labor, net financial results of fifth house affairs, foodstuffs, wearing apparel.

CORPORATION: Employees—including their character and health, corporation connection with hostelries, agriculture and agricultural products, working equipment, fixtures and furnishings.

*SEVENTH HOUSE:* International relations, including treaties; threats of war and overtures of peace; foreign trade; marriage and divorce, including civil suits opposed to popular opinion; opponents.

CORPORATION: Public accountings; adjustments; employee income and payrolls; volume of sales; best method of sales appeal.

*EIGHTH HOUSE:* Foreign finance, including effects of foreign exchange; financial results of treaties; the cabinet of the government; opposition to trade balances; national budget; flow of money; taxation; death rate.

CORPORATION: Credits; private conferences; all confidential information and trade secrets; the board of directors; net earnings.

*NINTH HOUSE:* The courts; legal, religious, philosophical and scientific developments; foreign trade and shipping; long distance travel; foreign news; insurance; resources of labor and the masses.

CORPORATION: Completion of contracts; litigation; audits; insurance; shipping; affiliations at a distance; inter-company correspondence.

*TENTH HOUSE:* The president or ruler; mayor of a city; political activity of the party in power; vested authority; business activity and turnover; leaders.

CORPORATION: The corporation head, or administrative department (note particularly the positions and aspects of the Sun); general business conditions; relations with government and associations.

*ELEVENTH HOUSE:* The Senate; The House of Representatives; financial results of government policies; money volume of business activity; legislation affecting business and government activity; government obligations; utilities.

CORPORATION: Corporation friends; resources of the head of the organization; political connections; constitutional policies; the good-will and intangible assets; indebtedness in bonds, mortgages, etc; treasurer.

*TWELFTH HOUSE:* All limitations, secrets, and moral obligations of government and business; the results of litigation; all public institutions such as reformatories, jails, hospitals and asylums; all speculative features involving eighth house affairs; all secret dealings involving the country.

CORPORATION: Experimentation and research; trade secrets, formulae and methods; limitations through secret enemies, including inefficiency; effects of litigation.

## KEY-WORDS FOR INTERPRETATION OF THE PLANETS

Sun (☉)—Government and administrators, authority, gold, speculation, theatre as a business, etc.

Moon ( ☽ )—Masses, crowds, crop harvests, popular ideas, sea, water.
Mercury ( ☿ )—Media, trade, commerce, publishing, advertising, doctors, printers, short travel.
Venus ( ♀ )—architecture, art, fashion, music halls, recreation.
Mars ( ♂ )—Army, Navy, surgeons, war, violence, epidemics, iron, steel, explosives, machinery, munitions, tobacco, sports.
Jupiter ( ♃ )—banking, brokers, courts, churches, favorable aspects abundance, unfavorable extravagance.
Saturn ( ♄ )—favorable aspects: patience, unfavorable: loss, depression; labor and laboring places, the land as of farms, grain, mines, real estate, mountainous places, the aged.
Uranus ( ♅ )—favorable aspects: change, unfavorable: disruptive; aircraft, electronics, railroads, tornadoes, strikes, radio energy, utilities, political socialism.
Neptune ( ♆ )—favorable aspects: creative, unfavorable: deception; actors, beverages, hospitals, bogus business operations, narcotics and drug companies, oil, photography, political idealism.
Pluto ( ♇ )—favorable aspects: cooperation, unfavorable: compulsion, dictatorships, atomic energy, plutonium, sewers, rackets, crime.
(The foregoing are samples of a wide range of applications; experience soon will suggest additions.)

ADDENDA 1978. Since publication of the foregoing in 1936 several new ephemerides have been developed and a wide exchange of books and magazines has taken place. In this situation American, British and Oriental studies use slightly different symbols from those most used in Continental Europe. For example, the Pluto symbol in European style seems to be a distorted Venus symbol of the American British form. Other sometimes disturbing differences appear in symbols for other planets. In this text symbols now growing in general acceptance are used. Note the often used symbol for Uranus, often mistaken for Neptune, is the European form. Unlike the symbol for Mars there is a dot in the ring and the stem is a vertical arrow.

CHAPTER FIVE

# ECLIPSES

One of the most important factors in mundane interpretation is to follow the effect of eclipses. Eclipses are most intense in their effects where they are visible. Sepharial's rule for finding the duration of the effects of an eclipse is: find the distance of the eclipsed luminary at conjunction or opposition from the Node. Then if 5° be divided by this distance, the magnitude of the eclipse will be obtained. Then for duration—as 1 is to 60, so is the magnitude to the number of months the eclipse will indicate. Thus:

| *Distance from Node* | *Magnitude* | *Years Duration* | *Months Duration* |
|---|---|---|---|
| ¼° | 20.00 | 100 | 0 |
| ½° | 10.00 | 50 | 0 |
| ¾° | 6.66 | 33 | 4 |
| 1° | 5.00 | 25 | 0 |
| 1¼° | 4.00 | 20 | 0 |
| 1½° | 3.33 | 16 | 8 |
| 1¾° | 2.857 | 14 | 3½ |
| 2° | 2.50 | 12 | 0 |
| 2¼° | 2.22 | 11 | 1 |
| 2½° | 2.00 | 10 | 0 |
| 2¾° | 1.818 | 8 | 4 |
| 3° | 1.67 | 7 | 8 |
| 3½° | 1.43 | 7 | 8 |
| 4° | 1.25 | 6 | 3 |
| 5° | 1.00 | 5 | 0 |
| 6° | .833 | 4 | 1½ |
| 8° | .625 | 3 | 1½ |
| 10° | .5 | 2 | 6 |
| 15° | .333 | 1 | 8 |

For interpretation of eclipses refer to "Eclipses in Theory and Practice" by Sepharial, and Raphael's "Mundane Astrology."

CHAPTER SIX

# INTERPRETATION OF THE PLANETS IN THE HOUSES AND SIGNS

When the student of astrology has mastered the mechanical phases of interpretation and begins to estimate the many influences involved in each chart many difficulties develop. A planet or house in one position is effective in a manner different from another position. The text-books contain tremendously voluminous tabulations of all the shades of meanings in each position, but then probably every possible meaning has never been in print. The whole problem of life and living is involved in a chart. Either more years of experience than can be crowded into one lifetime or a gargantuan memory would completely meet the problem. However, there is a simple way of getting into a chart, which does not attempt to tax the memory, and at the same time holds to simple first principles.

As discussed under Chapter One the Sun is attributed to rulership of the sign Leo, the fifth mundane house. The Sun's "personality" is colored by the fifth house influence but when it is in a chart its action depends on its sign position in relation to the sign Leo, with Leo as its first house. In other words the Sun in Leo is the Sun operating in a first house manner, but the Sun in Aquarius is the Sun operating in a seventh house manner—Aquarius being the 7th house from Leo. Now, in a radix the Sun may be in Leo in the 10th house. Then the Sun is operating in a first house manner through, or giving expression to this first house manner, the 10th house. In the same manner, Virgo is the first house of Mercury (it rules Virgo); then Mercury in Capricorn would be the Mercury nature or "personality" working in a fifth house manner, plus some of the eleventh house because it is the lower octave ruler of Gemini.

When the nature of each planet is learned, and the rulerships applied, a mental "key-word" system soon develops which quickly tabulates in the mind a large number of meanings to every planetary and sign position. Then if the text-books giving the multitudes of meanings are used, to build up a further understanding of specific meanings, progress can be made. The sooner a student is able to get away from reference works the better his ability of perception and interpretation becomes.

The basic texts for this are many. Alan Leo stressed this method of approaching what he called "memory co-ordination" but text-books apparently ignored the complete practicality of the point. However, recently Sidney K. Bennett developed several texts on interpretation along these lines which are of enormous interpretive value, to both the student and the professional, and decidedly worth their published price to both layman and student.

In mundane interpretation there is a great lack of reference material.

For general purposes Raphael's "Mundane Astrology" and A. J. Pearce's "Textbook of Astrology" are most useful.

In connection with planetary positions by both sign and house, detailed interpretation finds a tremendous source of help in taking cognizance of the fixed stars. Authoritative texts on this phase of the field are, "The Fixed Stars and Constellations" by Vivian E. Robson, and Johndro's "Stars"; "FIXED STARS and their interpretation" by Ebertin-Hoffman; English Edition published 1973 by Ebertin-Verlag.

CHAPTER SEVEN

# CASTING MUNDANE CHARTS

Mathematical precision to the second is not necessary in setting a geocentric chart of the heavens. Although there is no harm in computing every figure with the mathematical methods of an astronomical observatory the time consumed is far better placed on interpretation. A simple method of working is as follows. An ephemeris designed for astrological work for the years to be considered, a Tables of Houses, and blank chart forms are needed.

First, enter on the chart blank the house cusp degrees and signs.

This is done by converting the time data to standard time, if in daylight saving time; then find how far the location is in degrees from the nearest Standard Meridian Time Line. Add four minutes for each degree the location is East of that meridian, but subtract four minutes for each degree it is West (if West). The result is True Local Time.

In the ephemeris take the sidereal time for noon PREVIOUS to the chart location time and ADD:

(1) Sidereal Time for noon previous in ephemeris
(2) 10 seconds correction for every 15 degrees longitude
(3) The interval between previous noon and chart time
(4) 10 seconds correction for each hour of this period

The result is the sidereal Time of the chart.

Under the proper latitude in the Tables of Houses find that sidereal time which is closest to the sidereal time of the chart and from the Tables enter the signs and degrees on the proper house cusps of the chart.

Second, enter the planets in the houses of the chart.

Find Greenwich Mean Time by multiplying the degrees of longitude by 4 and divide by 60′, and add to the True Local Time, if West Longitude.

By logarithms, simple proportion, or preferably mathematical tables, compute the distance of travel of each planet since the Greenwich Time and zodiacal place shown in the ephemeris. Some ephemerides show the places of the planets at noon and some show them at midnight —make sure which.

Enter the computed positions in their proper places on the chart.

Third, compute the declinations and latitudes of each planet and tabulate these positions.

Fourth, tabulate all the major aspects in a speculum, and from the section of notes in this manual tabulate the natures and powers of each planet.

(Note: diurnal figures are cast according to Chapter Two)

CHAPTER EIGHT

# NOTES, BASE CHARTS, KEYS

The hundreds of volumes which have been consulted over a period of many years, combined with tests and practice of the many methods presented, has gradually evolved the material in this manual. The pages which follow are the framework of a ready reference note-book which is in daily use. The layman will find much of the data difficult to apply, but if the text-books referred to in the foregoing chapters are consulted the applications will be immediately made clear, for these notes are of valuable assistance.

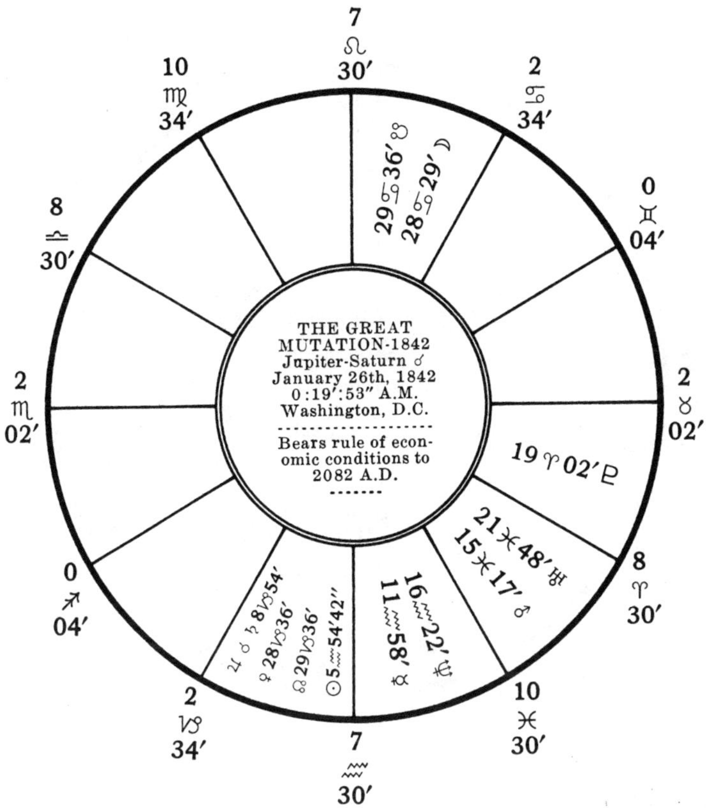
THE GREAT
MUTATION-1842
Jupiter-Saturn ☌
January 26th, 1842
0:19′:53″ A.M.
Washington, D.C.
Bears rule of economic conditions to
2082 A.D.
7 ♌ 30′
2 ♋ 34′
0 ♊ 04′
2 ♉ 02′
8 ♈ 30′
10 ♓ 30′
7 ♒ 30′
2 ♑ 34′
0 ♐ 04′
2 ♏ 02′
8 ♎ 30′
10 ♍ 34′
29♋36′☊
28♋29′☽
19♈02′♇
21♓48′♅
15♓17′♂
16♒22′♆
11♒58′☿
♃☌♄8♑54′
♀28♑36′
☋29♑36′
☉5♒54′42″

NOTES

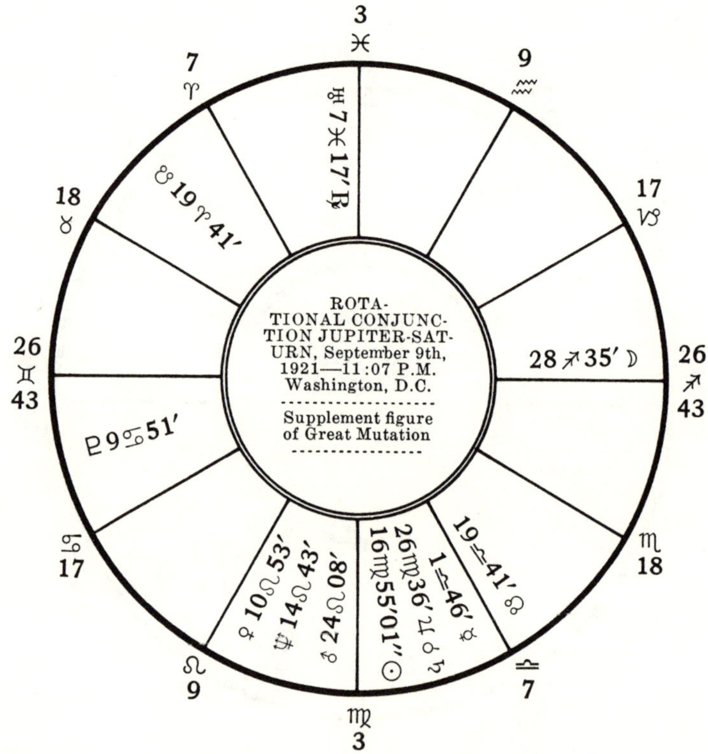
ROTATIONAL CONJUNCTION JUPITER-SATURN, September 9th, 1921—11:07 P.M. Washington, D.C.
Supplement figure of Great Mutation
♅ 7♓17′ ℞
☊ 19♈41′
28♐35′ ☽
♇ 9♋51′
♀ 10♌53′
♆ 14♌43′
♂ 24♌08′
16♍55′01″ ☉
26♍36′ ♃ ☌ ♄
1♎46′ ☿
19♎41′ ☋

NOTES

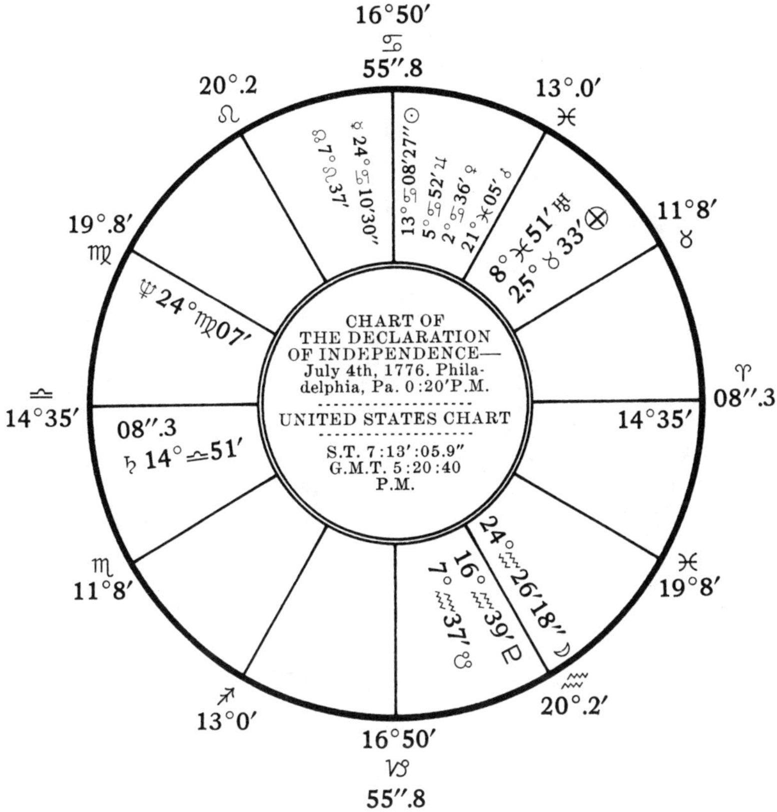
CHART OF
THE DECLARATION
OF INDEPENDENCE—
July 4th, 1776. Philadelphia, Pa. 0:20′P.M.
UNITED STATES CHART
S.T. 7:13′:05.9″
G.M.T. 5:20:40
P.M.
16°50′ ♋ 55″.8
13°.0′ ♓
11°8′ ♉
♈ 08″.3
14°35′
♓ 19°8′
♒ 20°.2′
16°50′ ♑ 55″.8
♐ 13°0′
♏ 11°8′
♎ 14°35′
08″.3
♄ 14°♎51′
19°.8′ ♍
20°.2 ♌
13°♋08′27″ ☉
5°♋52′ ♃
2°♋36′ ♀
21°♓05′ ♂
8°♓51′ ♅
25°♉33′ ⊕
♆ 24°♍07′
☿ 24°♋10′30″
☊ 7°♌37′
24°♒26′18″ ☽
16°♒39′ ♇
7°♒37′ ☋

NOTES

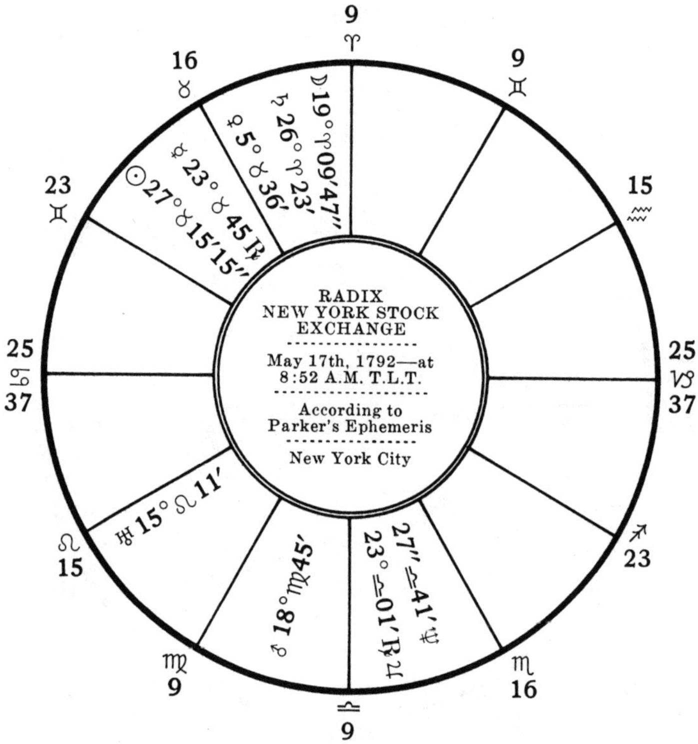
RADIX
NEW YORK STOCK EXCHANGE
May 17th, 1792—at 8:52 A.M. T.L.T.
According to Parker's Ephemeris
New York City

NOTES

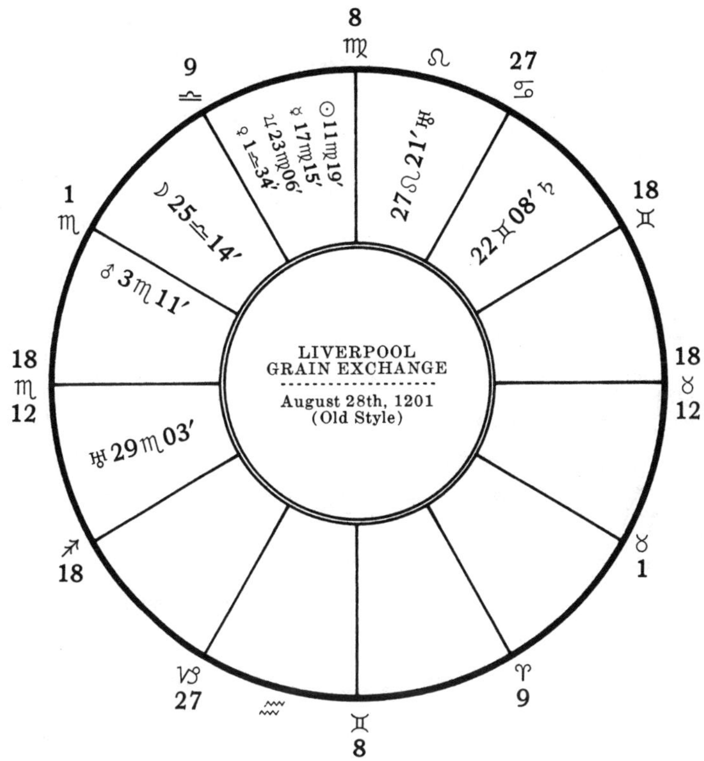
LIVERPOOL
GRAIN EXCHANGE
August 28th, 1201
(Old Style)
☉11♍19′
☿17♍15′
♃23♍06′
♀1♎34′
☽25♎14′
♂3♏11′
♅29♏03′
27♌21′♅
22♊08′♄
8 ♍
♌ 27 ♋
18 ♊
18 ♉ 12
♉ 1
♈ 9
♊ 8
♒
♑ 27
♐ 18
18 ♏ 12
1 ♏
9 ♎

## NOTES

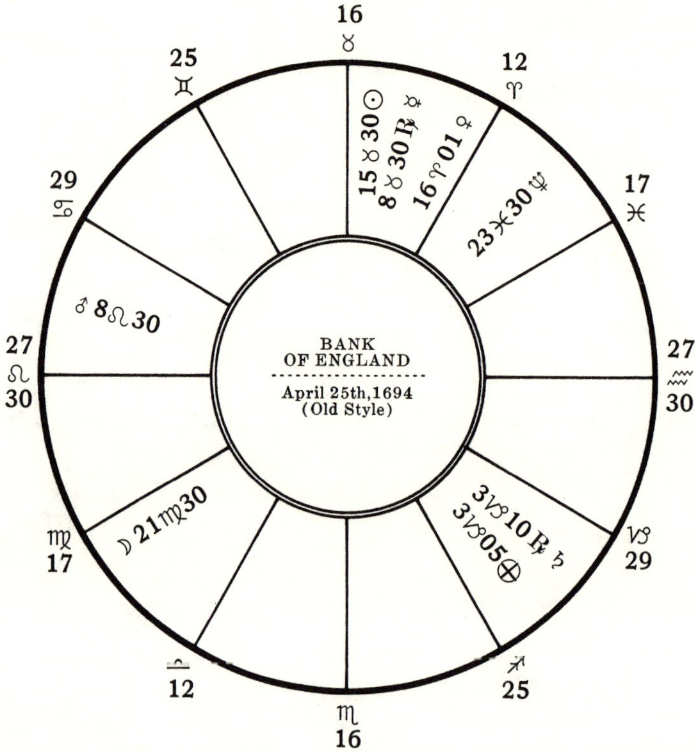


NOTES

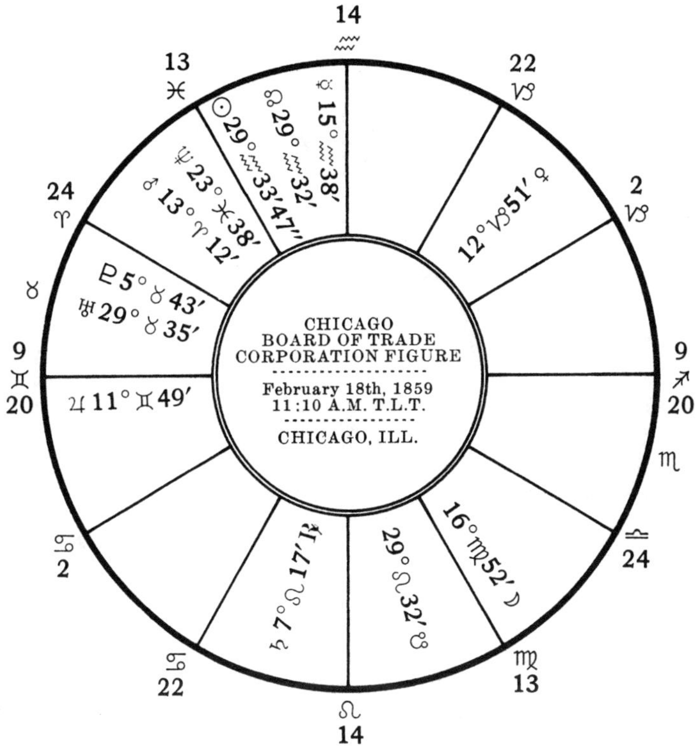
CHICAGO
BOARD OF TRADE
CORPORATION FIGURE
February 18th, 1859
11:10 A.M. T.L.T.
CHICAGO, ILL.

## NOTES

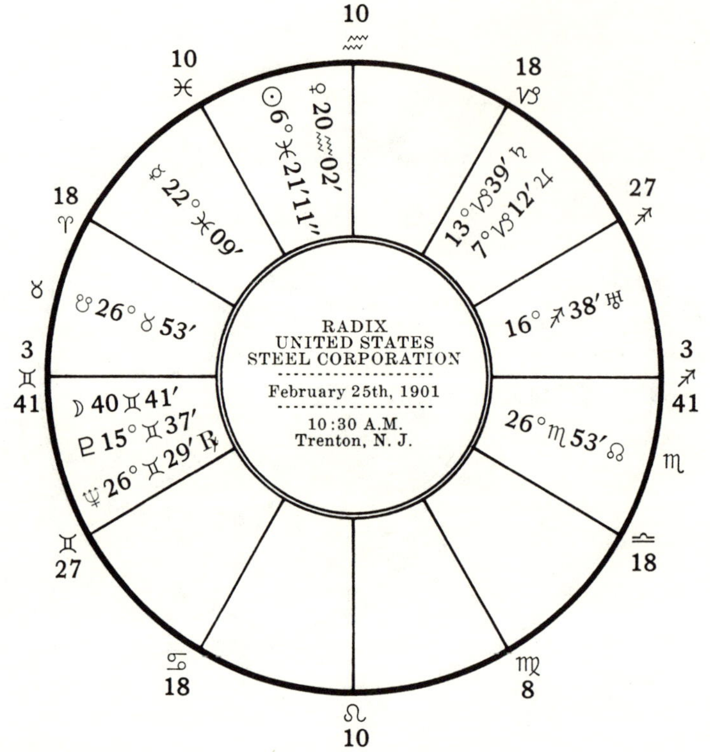
RADIX
UNITED STATES
STEEL CORPORATION
February 25th, 1901
10:30 A.M.
Trenton, N. J.
10 ♒
18 ♑
27 ♐
3 ♐ 41
♏
♎ 18
♍ 8
♌ 10
♋ 18
♊ 27
3 ♊ 41
♉
18 ♈
10 ♓
♀ 20 ♒ 02′
☉ 6° ♓ 21′11″
☿ 22° ♓ 09′
♄ 13° ♑ 39′
♃ 7° ♑ 12′
♅ 16° ♐ 38′
☊ 26° ♏ 53′
☋ 26° ♉ 53′
☽ 40 ♊ 41′
♇ 15° ♊ 37′
♆ 26° ♊ 29′ ℞

NOTES

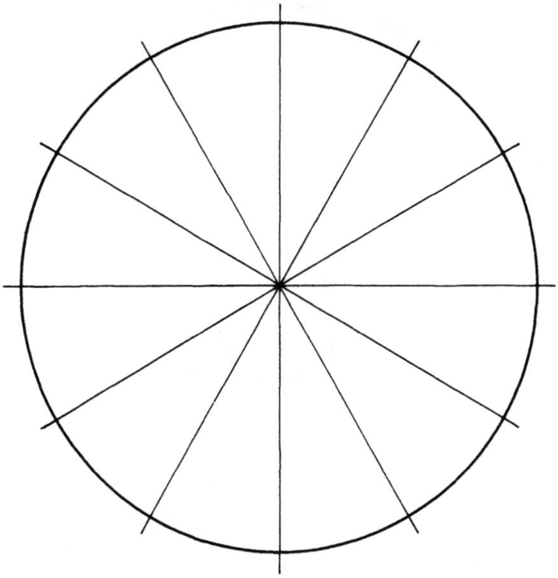

NOTES

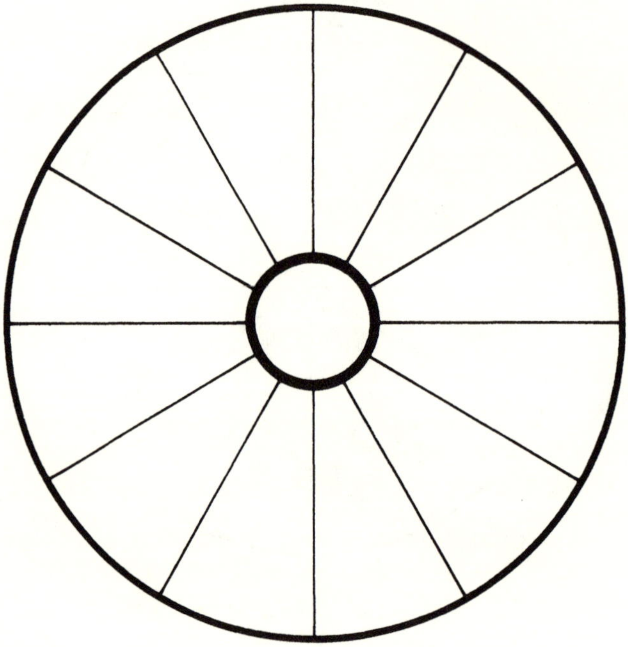

NOTES

### THE PLANETS

Sun—☉ Moon—☽ Mercury—☿
Venus—♀ Earth—⊕ Mars—♂
Jupiter—♃ Saturn—♄ Uranus—♅
Neptune—♆ Pluto—♇

### THE SIGNS

Aries—♈ Taurus—♉ Gemini—♊
Cancer—♋ Leo—♌ Virgo—♍
Libra—♎ Scorpio—♏ Sagittarius—♐
Capricorn—♑ Aquarius—♒ Pisces—♓

### PLANETARY AND SIGN NATURES

CARDINAL SIGNS—Aries, Cancer, Libra, and Capricorn
FIXED SIGNS—Taurus, Leo, Scorpio, and Aquarius
COMMON SIGNS—Gemini, Virgo, Sagittarius, and Pisces

FIRE SIGNS—Aries, Leo, and Sagittarius
EARTH SIGNS—Taurus, Virgo, and Capricorn
AIR SIGNS—Gemini, Libra, and Aquarius
WATER SIGNS—Cancer, Scorpio, and Pisces

POSITIVE SIGNS—Aries, Gemini, Leo, Libra, Sagittarius, and Aquarius
NEGATIVE SIGNS—Taurus, Cancer, Virgo, Scorpio, Capricorn, and Pisces (Positive signs are masculine, negative are feminine)

BARREN SIGNS—Aries, Gemini, Leo, and Virgo
FRUITFUL SIGNS—Taurus, Cancer, Scorpio, Sagittarius, and Pisces
INDIFFERENT SIGNS—Libra, Capricorn, and Aquarius

### PLANETARY POWERS

| *Planet* | *Rules* | *Detriment* | *Exaltation* | *Fall* |
|---|---|---|---|---|
| SUN— | ♌ | ♒ | ♈ | ♎ |
| VENUS— | ♉♎ | ♏♈ | ♓ | ♍ |
| MERCURY— | ♊♍ | ♐♓ | ♍ | ♌ |
| MOON— | ♋ | ♑ | ♉ | ♏ |
| SATURN— | ♑ | ♋ | ♎ | ♈ |
| JUPITER— | ♐ | ♊ | ♋ | ♑ |
| MARS— | ♈(♏) | ♎(♉) | (♑) | (♋) |
| URANUS— | ♒ | ♌ | ♏ | ♉ |
| NEPTUNE— | ♓ | ♍ | ♋ | ♑ |
| PLUTO— | ♈ | ♎ | ♑ | ♋ |

### PLANETARY REVOLUTIONS

Earth—365 days 7 hours
Moon—28 Days around earth
Mercury—88 days
Venus—224 days
Mars—1 year 322 days
Jupiter—11 years 322 days
Saturn—29 years 167 days
Uranus—84 years
Neptune—164 years 167 days

### DECANATE SIGN DIVISIONS

| DECAN | ♈ | ♉ | ♊ | ♋ | ♌ | ♍ | ♎ | ♏ | ♐ | ♑ | ♒ | ♓ |
|---|---|---|---|---|---|---|---|---|---|---|---|---|
| 0°-10° | ♈ | ♉ | ♊ | ♋ | ♌ | ♍ | ♎ | ♏ | ♐ | ♑ | ♒ | ♓ |
| 11°-20° | ♌ | ♍ | ♎ | ♏ | ♐ | ♑ | ♒ | ♓ | ♈ | ♉ | ♊ | ♋ |
| 21°-30° | ♐ | ♑ | ♒ | ♓ | ♈ | ♉ | ♊ | ♋ | ♌ | ♍ | ♎ | ♏ |

| DECAN | ♈ | ♉ | ♊ | ♋ | ♌ | ♍ | ♎ | ♏ | ♐ | ♑ | ♒ | ♓ |
|---|---|---|---|---|---|---|---|---|---|---|---|---|
| 0° - 10° | ♂ | ♀ | ☿ | ☽ | ☉ | ☿ | ♀ | ♂ | ♃ | ♄ | ♅ | ♆ |
| 11° - 20° | ☉ | ☿ | ♀ | ♂ | ♃ | ♄ | ♅ | ♆ | ♂ | ♀ | ☿ | ☽ |
| 21° - 30° | ♃ | ♄ | ♅ | ♆ | ♂ | ♀ | ☿ | ☽ | ☉ | ☿ | ♀ | ♂ |

DECANATE PLANETARY RULERSHIPS

### CRITICAL DEGREES

(Planets or house cusps in these degrees have intensified effects)

Aries 1°, 13°, 26°.
Taurus 9°, 21°.
Gemini 4°, 17°.
Cancer 1°, 13°, 26°.
Leo 9°, 21°.
Virgo 4°, 17°.

Libra 1°, 13°, 26°.
Scorpio 9°, 21°.
Sagittarius 4°, 17°.
Capricorn 1°, 13°, 26°.
Aquarius 9°, 21°.
Pisces 4°, 17°.

### PLANETARY TIME PERIODS

Moon—4 years
Mercury—10 years
Venus—8 years
Sun—19 years
Mars—15 years
Jupiter—12 years
Saturn—40 years
Uranus—90 years
Neptune—180 years

### TO CALCULATE THE PART OF FORTUNE

Add to the Longitude of the Moon the Longitude of the Ascendant and subtract the longitude of the Sun from the total.

### TO CALCULATE GREENWICH MEAN TIME FOR ANY POINT WEST LONGITUDE

Add four minutes for each degree of longitude the location is WEST of Greenwich to the true local time at the location.

### TO CALCULATE TRUE LOCAL TIME

To the nearest Standard Meridian Time, ADD four minutes for each degree the location is EAST of the Meridian corresponding to that time. If the location is WEST of that Meridian, SUBTRACT four minutes for each degree it is WEST thereof.

### TO CALCULATE THE ADJUSTED CALCULATION DATE

(for secondary directions)

(a) Compute the interval from G. M. T. to following noon

(b) To this interval add the Sidereal Time for G. M. T. noon on the radix day—this equals the Sidereal Time of the Adj. Calcu. Date.

(c) If the G. M. T. falls in the A.M.—count forward in the ephemeris.

(d) If the G. M. T. falls in the P.M., or in the A.M. of the next day, count backwards.

### TO ADJUST CUSPS FOR A POINT REMOTE FROM THE RADIX LOCATION

To the Sidereal Time of the radix, if the direction be EAST, ADD—if the direction be WEST, SUBTRACT—the difference in longitude, reduced to hours and minutes. With this new Sidereal Time the house cusps of the new location are taken from the Tables of Houses. The planets are inserted in the same zodiacal signs, degrees and minutes as in the radix chart. A new Part of Fortune position is calculated according to the revised Ascendant.

### TO PROGRESS A RADIX FIGURE WHEN AN EPHEMERIS IS NOT AVAILABLE

(Note section on Progressions and Transits in this manual)

| *Years* | *Arc* | *Months* | *Arc* | *Days* | *Arc* |
|---|---|---|---|---|---|
| 1 | 0 59′ 08″ | 1 | 4′ 45″ | 1 | 0′ 10″ |
| 2 | 1 58′ 17″ | 2 | 9′ 51″ | 2 | 0′ 20″ |
| 3 | 2 57′ 25″ | 3 | 14′ 47″ | 3 | 0′ 30″ |
| 4 | 3 56′ 33″ | 4 | 19′ 43″ | 4 | 0′ 39″ |
| 5 | 4 55′ 42″ | 5 | 24′ 38″ | 5 | 0′ 49″ |
| 6 | 5 54′ 50″ | 6 | 29′ 34″ | 6 | 0′ 59″ |
| 7 | 6 53′ 58″ | 7 | 34′ 30″ | 7 | 1′ 09″ |
| 8 | 7 53′ 07″ | 8 | 39′ 26″ | 8 | 1′ 19″ |
| 9 | 8 52′ 15″ | 9 | 44′ 21″ | 9 | 1′ 29″ |
| 10 | 9 51′ 23″ | 10 | 49′ 17″ | 10 | 1′ 39″ |

Compute Moon's rate: 13° 10′ 35″ per year

### MUNDANE PLANETARY HOUSES BY PLANETS

Aries is the first sign of the zodiac and occupies the first house in the natural zodiac. Its ruler is Mars. Therefore no matter where Mars falls in a radix figure it exerts a first house influence. In the same way, Venus ruling Taurus the second natural zodiacal sign is a financial and second house influence; Mercury, ruling Gemini, is a third house influence, etc.

| SIGN | ♈ | ♉ | ♊ | ♋ | ♌ | ♍ | ♎ | ♏ | ♐ | ♑ | ♒ | ♓ |
|---|---|---|---|---|---|---|---|---|---|---|---|---|
| RULER | ♂ | ♀ | ☿ | ☽ | ☉ | ☿ | ♀ | ♂ | ♃ | ♄ | ♅ | ♆ |
| HOUSE | 1 | 2 | 3 | 4 | 5 | 6 | 7 | 8 | 9 | 10 | 11 | 12 |

### MUNDANE PLANETARY HOUSES BY SIGNS

Mars, (self, aggression, etc) a first house influence, when located in Taurus (the natural second sign), exerts its first house influence in a second house or money and finance manner. The selfness and aggressiveness of a Mars in Aries becomes (in Taurus) money aggression. In a mundane radix figure this position, for illustration, might appear in the fifth house. This would presage (Mars in Taurus in the 5th) money aggression through speculative (5th) channels involving agriculture, real estate, and mines (With the sign Taurus on the fifth cusp, Aries—ruled by Mars—would be on the 4th)

The key to the entire planetary house pattern is as follows:

| | ♂ | ♀ | ☿ | ☽ | ☉ | ☿ | ♀ | ♂ | ♃ | ♄ | ♅ | ♆ |
|---|---|---|---|---|---|---|---|---|---|---|---|---|
| ♈ | 1 | 12 | 11 | 10 | 9 | 8 | 7 | 6 | 5 | 4 | 3 | 2 |
| ♉ | 2 | 1 | 12 | 11 | 10 | 9 | 8 | 7 | 6 | 5 | 4 | 3 |
| ♊ | 3 | 2 | 1 | 12 | 11 | 10 | 9 | 8 | 7 | 6 | 5 | 4 |
| ♋ | 4 | 3 | 2 | 1 | 12 | 11 | 10 | 9 | 8 | 7 | 6 | 5 |
| ♌ | 5 | 4 | 3 | 2 | 1 | 12 | 11 | 10 | 9 | 8 | 7 | 6 |
| ♍ | 6 | 5 | 4 | 3 | 2 | 1 | 12 | 11 | 10 | 9 | 8 | 7 |
| ♎ | 7 | 6 | 5 | 4 | 3 | 2 | 1 | 12 | 11 | 10 | 9 | 8 |
| ♏ | 8 | 7 | 6 | 5 | 4 | 3 | 2 | 1 | 12 | 11 | 10 | 9 |
| ♐ | 9 | 8 | 7 | 6 | 5 | 4 | 3 | 2 | 1 | 12 | 11 | 10 |
| ♑ | 10 | 9 | 8 | 7 | 6 | 5 | 4 | 3 | 2 | 1 | 12 | 11 |
| ♒ | 11 | 10 | 9 | 8 | 7 | 6 | 5 | 4 | 3 | 2 | 1 | 12 |
| ♓ | 12 | 11 | 10 | 9 | 8 | 7 | 6 | 5 | 4 | 3 | 2 | 1 |

CHAPTER NINE

# THE UNITED STATES BIRTH CHART

A basic premise of astro computation procedures is precise timing as mandatory before accurate interpretation can occur. It is only by charting the exact moment of the first breath of a child at birth registers the implications of the lifetime which follows. In much the same tradition the birth or beginning of a business plan or project, a company or a nation often reveals future successes, dangers and disasters. Many entire lifetimes have been spent devising, guessing, testing chart times of beginnings.

A major example in the past 50 years has been the United States birth, with controversy and almost endless debate over what is the correct birth chart. Such debates are good exercises in research but none of them are of value in actual financial decisions. Many years ago a very earnest researcher came to me with a record of transits to the position of the Moon in the July 4th, 1776 United States Chart. Hindsight seemed to prove specific market action for years in the past with this system. A new convergence was to occur in a matter of weeks. It failed completely.

The location of the Moon is one position in the Noon or Libra Rising chart at the left. This figure long was accepted as official inasmuch as the Declaration of Independence got its last signature about 11:20 A.M. and the official public announcing, by a Town Crier, was a few minutes after 12 noon. But critics rose to attack the time of the chart. Libra Rising with Saturn were not the image or American spirit, or so their interpretation methods claimed.

In research bulletins of the American Academy of Astrologians, subsequently amplified in my articles in the ASTROLOGICAL BULLETINA, and then presented in the chapter on The Uranus Cycle, the key was the 7th to 9th degrees of Gemini. Uranus was crossing this area on July 4th, 1776, just as it had done at the forming of the first colony by the Spanish in 1523, again in the formation of the Jamestown Colony in 1607, and the timing of the 1691 Revolution.

Due principally to this observation opinion began to use 2:19 A.M. July 4th, 1776 as the chart time for the USA birth. It placed Uranus exactly on the Ascendant and the M. C. in Aquarius with the Moon nearly conjunct in the 10th house. No longer was the Moon in 24° but at 18°, promptly ruining the mass of doctrine on progressions, etc. Students who have spent 25 years and often far much less in astro research study currently boldly proclaim this early morning chart as the Gemini figure and authentic key to the USA for the past, present and future. Arguments are endless but the innovative, compassionate, science aspiring Uranus on an Ascendant is more romantic than a cautious, systematic, thrifty Saturn.

For years members of the Continental Congress discussed preparation of a formal statement of principles. The formation of a committee of three was authorized the morning of June 10th, 1776 to draw up a declaration to be submitted to the Congress. Thomas Jefferson did the actual writing which the committee presented. When was the initial idea born? But it is historical fact the people of the 13 colonies learned that independence, probable war and internal dissension became official in a do or die decision about noon.

In the chart for noon Saturn is a key. As Llewellyn George often said to me "Saturn is discipline, tenacity, just and tinged with puritanism; but it has a bad name as reaper and depressant of excesses." The most cursory examination of the transits of Saturn in the Libra Rising chart through the 9th, 10th and 11th Houses in American history is a clock, timing problems. When Saturn has been aspected by other slow moving planet positions at each of these periods the effects are specific. The phenomena may be now traced back for two centuries for confirmation. One obvious example was in the years immediately following 1929. Foreign affairs in the 1920's had been beyond the capacities of private enterprise credit and financial resources and the confidence which accrued. A major effect of the 1929 crash was mortgage foreclosures on a broad scale. Reference to page 39 of section II lists house meanings. In 1930 expansive and optimistic Jupiter was at the MC of the USA Libra chart reflecting business activity, vested authority, etc, opposed by Saturn the reaper and depresser at the cusp of the 4th house (real property, tangible assets, anti-optimistic vested authority, etc). To compound this stern indication was the square of Uranus near a conjunction with Mars near the cusp of the 7th house (foreign relations, foreign trade, worker income and payrolls, sales volume of business, etc.). This forms a devestating negative situation and for the USA notably severe. The first signs of any relief did not appear until the second quarter of 1932 with the initial financial recovery apparent as of July 9th under the trine of Jupiter and Uranus with Saturn weak and retrograde in Aquarius.

Comparable inspections may be made from an ephemeris of the year involved and planetary positions compared. Use aspect interaction and the related USA Libra chart positions according to planet meanings on page 49. Admittedly this is a very simple approach, but effective. Next then is ignore for the moment any "birth" such as the foregoing USA figure. In 1930 Jupiter moved into the sign of Cancer at mid-year. On page 59 the horizontal column lists Jupiter as ruling the sign Sagittarius. In the columns covering page 60 Jupiter in Cancer is Jupiter's 8th house position. Under 8th house on page 40 an 8th house Jupiter centers attention to foreign finances, money flow, credit, etc. When in this Cancer sign position an opposition from Saturn plus the square of Uranus forms an ominous economic portent. The situation continued in an unrelenting fashion and then worsened as the Moon's Node neared a conjunction with Uranus to magnify the effects of the stellium of Uranus, Saturn and Jupiter.

As noted on page 58 Jupiter makes its full circle approximately every

12 years. A return to the sign Cancer, for an example of a different climate than the early 1930's, was in 1954. The nation, in fact the world, had struggled through the ruins of World War II and seemed to have contrived a foundation for renewed growth. People generally were discouraged and doggedly hoping for better things but were at low ebb in 1953 (Saturn in conjunction with Neptune in Libra squared by Uranus in the sign Cancer.). However, in 1954 Jupiter moved into Cancer while Saturn shifted into the sign Scorpio (a trine). The Uranus Neptune square aspect activated inflated credits in its release from Saturn, while the Moon's Node was sextile Neptune. The belated secondary post-war boom was underway. Serious exhaustion did not develop until late in 1965 although reactions and readjustments appeared in 1957, 1960 and 1962. Examination of those years in terms of the foregoing methods may prove a valuable investment in interpretation skills.

(N. B. In your initial examination—using only the ephemeris for the years involved, make note of the sign-house of each planet, viz Neptune in Libra is its 8th; Saturn in Libra its 10th. Thus Neptune in its sign-house 8th reflects unlimited aspirations for money in co-operative plans with others. Uranus Cancer is Uranus 6th sign-house denoting public spending for military, public works, ecology, nurture of labor & agriculture.)

The ultimate in interpretation tools is found in proven "birth" time as chart formations with the location usually the capital of a country. But for serious mundane conclusions charts erected for each quarterly ingress a year and all the lunations are useful. Locations selected depend on the subject matter. Here is a juncture where a maze of computations and stacks of charts can form which defeats the basic study: direct and simple means of aiding a conclusion without nit-picking the impossible.

Often it is sad and very wry to read or hear about some group of scholars, economists and statisticians had compiled masses of data which programmed a huge computer. The answer was that employment would increase and in another period of so many months unemployment would shrink to so much. It is all very well but grasp the time and efforts involved to conclude these generalizations. Your batting average may never be 100% but with some time and concerted effort it can be far ahead of the pro group. Of course, we also have to be realistic in realizing the majority only listen to what it wants to hear and what fits their hopes or misgivings at the time.

Forecast a probable boom and no one believes it. When it occurs they say they are sorry they didn't listen. Forecast an economic or market peak and a barrage of quotes that so and so, or this and that source, states things are going much higher. Then remorse when the peak is confirmed no action was taken. But that is the way of life; people working out their own bumbling destiny the hard way and often to die in frustration and considerable despair. Generally denied only a very few exert the effort and stamina to find Nature's immutable laws and actually heed them. Only very bad forecasts, which are from 50 to 100% wrong, are generally heeded as they seem to have the profound ability to get into print and be widely quoted. A person has to dig out his own progress if it is to be lasting. It can open up extraordinary opportunities.

Learn through texts the inherent qualities and features of each planet as experienced from ancient times. Expansive and generally benefic by themselves are Jupiter and Venus; Mars vigorous, aggressive, forceful, etc. And the angular relations are extremely significant. Briefly, two classes of angles dominate; one is the 90° span of 90, 45, 22½, etc; the other the 120° group of 120, 60, 30, 15, etc. Sometimes both occur interlocked at one time such as 3 15's making a 45. These related degrees are, with inherent planet qualities, intensely important and often supersede the various complete chart figures.

Close grasp of the significance and operation of angular relationships are very important. In the concluding section of this work these angles become the foundation of the program used to define probable market trends as to prices and timing of swings and probable amplitude, using the daily, weekly and monthly price ranges of stocks and commodities.

The preceding two sections—major cyclic trends and cyclic interpretation factors—are a simplified foundation for the real goal of workable methods.

CHAPTER TEN

# AN "OVER"—SIMPLIFIED METHOD OF ASTRO-CYCLE INTERPRETATION

Traditionalists call for the erection of astro chart figures based on a precise time and place. For mundane subjects such as business and market trends this means charting the exact time of the four quarterly Ingresses of the Sun as each quarter-year begins. The place is the locality considered the center of the subject such as a national capital. Supplementing the Ingress figures are each New Moon, and sometimes each Moon Quarter. This practice is mandatory for precise results.

The new student trying to get into the field without the tedium of perhaps months of study may find this simple method encouraging and profitable, and ignore tradition.

The initial requirement is an ephemeris for the period to be studied. The immediate and current year usually contains the interest. A geocentric ephemeris is needed; this is a revised version of the official heliocentric ephemeris issued by a number of governments for military, naval and other astronomical applications. As we are interested in the effects of solar and other cosmic radiation and reflective rays on the Earth a heliocentric (Sun as center of the angular relationships) ephemeris would be a distortion from the standpoint of the Earth.

Most complete ephemeris is RAPHAEL'S for the year desired. Published in London for a century it is available for about $3 a copy through most bookshops. More available and in a simple format is the Rosicrucian Fellowship Ephemeris, P. O. Box 713, Oceanside, Calif. 92054 at $1.50 for each year desired. (Note: although not used in this simple method later work will require a Table of Houses. Several are available with the most economical and simple to use is that of the Rosicrucian Fellowship. The various blank forms may be deferred.)

Instead of theorizing let us take an example and work on it as an illustration you can check out for yourself. It is the afternoon of August 1st, 1976. Current newspapers and business magazines are chortling over bullish trends. Opinion seems general things are consolidating for a long boom. The statistics continue to reflect steady gains since the upswing began in early 1975 in business and the low of stocks late in 1974. Very nice! We can go back to sleep, buy more stocks and continue to rake in the business as things are better than they were and are all set to be better for a long time ahead!! Typical? Yes, and usually wrong.

So get a sheet of paper, a pencil or a pen that writes an original, and that ephemeris for the year 1976 and August. On the 1st we find funny looking things heading columns of figures. We want the page carrying DECLINATION OF THE PLANETS.

Out of this apparent maze of columns we shall only check three:

| | | | |
|---|---|---|---|
| Uranus | (♅) | 3 Scorpio | (♏) |
| Saturn | (♄) | 6 Leo | (♌) |
| Jupiter | (♃) | 27 Taurus | (♉) |

> Taurus in the zodiac circle is opposition (180°) Scorpio and square (90°) Leo. This means that Leo is square both Taurus and Scorpio.

In the above Jupiter has small potency as it is not "in orb" to Uranus and Saturn, but the latter are in orb. Taking the three as a unit the news reports and forecasts are "whistling in the dark to bolster their spirits." The foundation is precarious.

Reference 60 Section II Jupiter in Taurus (♃ ♉) is a 6th sign house in a 2nd house sign; our notes show this involves money for national health and safety (it could refer to vaccine, relief from flood) but also an unusual demand for money by organized workers.

Next, the Uranus in Scorpio (♅ ♏) again refer to page 60; an 8th sign house in a 10th sign house suggests a large number of public policies are viewed as irrational in matters of spending and taxation, foreign affairs, currency and foreign exchange.

And last, Saturn in Leo (♄ ♌) a 5th house sign in an 8th sign house. National apprehension over children and their lack of freedom of choice in education, low standards of public morality, debate on national budgets and taxes, lack of financial speculative confidence.

The only action in this three-way is Saturn (curtailment, discipline) is directly in mutual assault with Uranus (innovation, impulsive, emotional) and with Jupiter momentarily inactive (out of orb) we have a nation confined largely to routine pursuits. It seems to reflect the early August state due to the political situation. The same forces affect other nations; various degree of turmoil, revolution, war and war threats are occurring in Asia, Africa and Middle-East.

As the newspapers report, the statistics are good; but the astro-cycle data state it is a neutral and precarious situation. Conclusion: it is a period for caution. For the probable time and direction of change we examine Jupiter's pattern several months from now. Then the basis of a forecast will begin to form.

In the astro-cycle data the obvious basis for the upswing in the stock market from mid-1970 (the very favorable aspects between Jupiter, Saturn and Uranus) was due to subside as sign changes developing in the last half of 1972 neutralized the bullish psychology. The Transport Average tried a new high in the second quarter (1972) to broach the preceding triple highs of 1966, 1967 and 1968–9 but failed by a fraction and declined. But the Industrial Average continued strong and surmounted their preceding 1966 and 1968 highs until January 1973 when weakness took hold. Jupiter in Capricorn formed a conjunctions with the Moon's Node and a full square (90°) to Uranus in Libra while Saturn was retrograde and neutral in Gemini. In January the Transport Average broke the preceding low in October and implied a bear market, although full confirmation of the Transports by the Industrials did not occur until November 1973. This established a very bearish market climate for 1974.

Historically this has become an unusual area of national economic affairs. Peculiar intrusions into supply-demand factors of commodities and the export markets with unprecedented price distortions were dwarfed by revelations which ruined the Administrative branch of government. In our "over"-simplified astro-cycle examination for 1974 we find the Moon's Node in Sagittarius with Saturn in opposition (180°). Then in April Saturn moved from Gemini into Cancer (this crosses the Mid-Heaven of the July 4th, 1776 U. S. Chart) the 4th House Sign and 7th Sign House working toward the square (90°) relation to Uranus in Libra (7th House Sign, 9th Sign House).

By September 1974 stock market liquidation became rampant, despite a weak (retrograde) Jupiter forming a trine angle to Saturn, as both the Moon's Node and Uranus remained virtually unchanged. Then, late in November, Uranus moved into Scorpio and conditions changed. By mid-December Jupiter was direct again, moving toward a trine with Saturn, which was beginning to get the effects of a growing trine from Uranus. To strengthen the pattern the Moon's Node reached a climax by crossing opposite the 9th degree of Gemini, with a sextile from Pluto which was trine the 9° of Gemini. This was the spot for a massive low in the stock market for a recovery of at least 15 to 18 months.

If careful study of the foregoing three paragraphs in relation to the ephemerides for the years is made by the notes of the economic keywords, the technique should become clear. But you are stymied by some factors not mentioned in the examples. They involve the Moon's Node, Pluto and the Jupiter-Saturn link.

In Section I the discussion on the twenty-year cycle was the periodic conjunctions of Jupiter and Saturn. For more than 100 years of business and investment market statistics, beginning in 1812, the booms and depressions were geared to the angular relation of Jupiter and Saturn. An enormous amount of time and expense was applied to collect the data and public records earlier than 1897. The relationship was further explored in the 1930's and presented in a book by James Mars Langham.

CHAPTER ELEVEN

# THE ASPECTS OR ANGLES BETWEEN PLANETS

The 360° circle of the astro chart is divided into twelve segments of 30° each. These segments are the signs. Their significance forms a division: four signs are cardinal, four are fixed and four are mutable; and another division of three Fire, three Earth, three Air and three Water. The first forms a triangle visually and the second group a square when drawn on the 12 segment circle. Thus, planet aspects are of two groups, the square and the triangle or trine.

There is the conjunction or 0° in both groups. The square group includes: the semi-square or 45° (∠), the square or 90° (□), the sesquiquadrate or 135° (⚼) which is 90° plus 45°, and the opposition or 180° (☍). Generally all are unfavorable.

The trine group has the conjunction under certain conditions, the semi-sextile or 30° (⚺), the sextile or 60° (⚹), the trine or 120° (△) and the quincunx or inconjunct or 150° (△). Parallels (||) depend on the plants involved.

In market trend interpretation the squares generally are bearish, the trines bullish. Again there are circumstances when such an arbitrary rule does not apply. There are specific answers to such problems but things become rather involved in more advance studies involving sign location of a planet and its Detriment, Exaltation, Fall, Critical degree and Orb of Aspect. And expecting precise action, such as a market peak, at the day and hour an aspect becomes exact, may fail. Often the reason is that an orb of aspect should be allowed, about 2 to 5% usually is generous, PLUS a trigger. A trigger is a fast moving planet coming into the major aspect, particularly Mars, sometimes Mercury. Hindsight will discover it on study from which experience will develop so advance interpretation can take place. No two situations ever are alike.

The conjunctions of Jupiter and Saturn were but a small part of defining market trends. But when the various aspects noted in the foregoing are followed in the ephemeris of the statistics of the year being examined the parallel between planetary aspects and the statistical trends soon takes form.

In the 1930's and 1940's this usual pattern began to break up. Disconcerting lags began to appear; most data was failing. Examination found Uranus aspects becoming potent. Some of the phenomena of the Uranus 84 year cycle was detailed in Section I. As time went on it was found that the shift of economic and money power from private forces to the budding Washington Bureaucracy was developing a new set of rules. Private Capitalism and Free Enterprise were more and more coming under political control through rules of a bureaucratic structure. It was the principal index to the panic liquidation of 1973 and 1974 discussed in the foregoing. To the almost perfect score presented by James Mars Langham on the interaction of Jupiter and Saturn in business and finance for over a century it has been more complicated since World War II.

Another useful factor applied to the interpretive procedures in the foregoing is to use the cycle data of the Moon's Node.

The symbol in the ephemeris of the Moon's Node is ( ☊ ). Other nodes exist but we shall ignore them at this time. This Moon's Node we mention is more exactly the Moon's North Node. It regresses (counter-clockwise instead of the clockwise movement of the planets) and makes the full circle in about 6 months more than 18 years—for our purpose call it 18 years.

Using that unexplained and unique North American continental point of 7°–9° Gemini as zero or starting point an unusual business cycle cadence again appears. It seems to intensify and at times cushion the interaction patterns of Jupiter, Saturn and Uranus. (Note: recall it was shown how potent this zero node point was in the timing of the Uranus cycle, for example the timing of the first settlement in 1523, etc.)

Application of the aspects, both bearish and bullish, to the Moon's Node in the ephemeris for each year, and using the Gemini point as the conjunction on which to form sextiles, squares, trines, etc, the major market trend takes form. The squares approximate major lows. But lows after sextiles differ in intensity than lows after trines. In 1976 there is a quincunx or inconjunct following an opposition. Squares for the lows in this particular cycle were early 1961, 1970 and 1979. For study it is suggested, beginning with the square following the sextile in 1932, process each year of the stock market with the Moon's Node aspects in order to grasp the method yourself.

Another element in our chain of factors is the probable effects of Pluto. Relatively new in tracing its probable use it appears to intrude underworld thinking related to autocratic power ranging from gang warfare to misuse of established authority. It has generally been assigned to rule the sign Scorpio. This bears very careful scrutiny. For many reasons having no place for discussion here it seems to relate more to Aries than Scorpio. Debate is unnecessary but in defining situations where Pluto is prominent consider the Aries climate. Incidentally for a long, long time Mars has been assigned to rule Aries AND Scorpio, with Pluto assigned as co-ruler of Scorpio which is subject to doubt.

When some facility has been acquired in co-ordinating the planets in their House Signs, then their Sign Houses, their aspect relationships from the proper ephemeris, on your note pad, refer to the Keywords in the group arrangement which follows for your budding interpretation progress. In the course of time you then will want to cast complete charted figures using the Table of Houses already mentioned. Locations selected as mentioned also start with the Ingresses and then the Lunations.

CHAPTER TWELVE

# COMBINING SIGN-HOUSES WITH HOUSE-SIGNS AND ASPECTS

Trend conditions at any given time are vital in any investment action. If the major trend is upward investment hazards are minimal; making commitments in a major downward trend or during a rally correction in a downward trend can be hazardous. Let's try to illustrate a process by which circumstances can be defined. We select a memorable and most confused period.

In mid-May 1942 both the national and international situation was considerably mixed. The impact of an attack on Pearl Harbor in the preceding December had the domestic scene in a general state of feverish doubts. Turn to Raphael's ephemeris for 1942 and note May 15th. There was a lunation or New Moon at 5:45 A.M. GMT, but we will not plot it out at this point as too complicated. The individual planet positions have our attention.

Neptune ( ♆ ) in (♍) Virgo: 7th Sign-House in a 6th House-Sign, heavily afflicted (negative aspected). This reflects rumors, false and true; and a chaotic emotional state among the masses relating to Armed Services, food, clothing, jobs and the enemy. With a wide conjunction by Moon's Node, which is precisely square the critical national point of 9° Gemini ( ♊ ) which signals a classic low in economic trends, it can be a memorable point in history.

Uranus ( ♅ ) in 5th Sign-House and 3rd House-Sign, a general state of apparent disruption and seemingly chaotic situation in transportation, feverish attempts to coordinate plans and action by authority, which is downgraded by public emotions, as

Saturn ( ♄ ) in 6th Sign-House in 3rd House-Sign, is precisely at apparent conjunction with Uranus. The people (6th) and 3rd (communications, ideas) feel scared, uncertain, even licked. Briefly adding to the crisis is Mercury ( ☿ ) in its 1st and 4th Sign-Houses in the 3rd House-Sign, amplifying the foregoing and adding worry over property, crops, etc. And then Venus ( ♀ ) 12th Sign-House in 1st House-Sign in square aspect (unfavorable) to Mars in Cancer (♋) 4th Sign-House in 10th House-Sign. This latter hopes but distrusts national leadership; briefly void-of-course (without strong aspects) from the Sun-Moon conjunction.

If we think these notes on each planet through we realize the same vibrations are world-wide. Obviously the response varies from environment and location how each factor may be most dominant.

*Turn to the chapter on MUNDANE RULERSHIPS. The Raphael Ephemeris positions as of noon GMT May 15th, 1942 are entered in rulership charts set up for Washington, Tokyo, Berlin and London as*

*appended. Note all planet positions are alike but houses differ. The foregoing interpretation applies to all of them but the locality charts reflect enormous differences in the accents and psychology in each location.*

The London figure has an 11th house concentration which centers national affairs on government policies and finance, planning, legislation, business and national policies. Ruler of the 10th (leadership) in the Ascendant (the people) marks a belligerent unity with Venus in 10th enthusiasm; dogged will to come out on top.

Berlin differs little in problems and practice except Pluto is on the Ascendant (The People) reflecting a full dictatorship. The Venus to Pluto aspect is waning and past the MC; and square Mars dominates the 12th, amply reflecting a police state.

The Tokyo figure has leadership (10th) placed in 7th (foreign adversaries), indicated by the Sun, and most concentration on 7th house (foreign) affairs and 8th house (costs and plans of 7th). The people (Mars ruler of 1st and 6th) giving cooperation as the square of Venus is below the horizon confined to misgivings by youth and children. Neptune marks illusions of success while the Node in the 10th marks a feeling of well being.

The Washington chart has the Gemini concentration past the Nadir and working upward with all-out attention to planning, finance and all resources directed to (Saturn ruling 10th) conj. Uranus ruling 11th (legislation, etc) on longer term. Neptune in 6th allows unleashed rumors, but the people (Asc) are unifying (Venus Aries) with a spirit of willingness to fight in the streets (ruler of 1st at cusp of 4th), if necessary; a vigor is stirring.

This chart should be something of a classic. It marks most positions under the horizon (the low ebb of a cycle) but most positions rising (new beginnings). In the latter is the major conj. of Saturn-Uranus in Gemini with Mercury and Jupiter. If a nation, emotionally and physically, was ever lower it is hard to find. That it is a low is reflected by the Node precisely square its critical point at 9° Gemini FOLLOWING a Trine (this differs from a subsequent square following sextile by the Node).

---

As noted several times 7 to 9 degrees of Gemini mark a unique national hinge or critical point. The Node takes about 18½ years for a complete cycle, something over 9 years for each half. Its apparent motion is counter-clockwise. To further explore the background the England critical national point seems to work out at 14° of Gemini. Until recent years comment was constant that major British events always had a similar counterpart later in the United States. British devaluation, British stock market bear markets, British election upsets and some time later much the same appeared in American affairs. Usually it timed to the aspects to the Node critical points.

New Moon—May 15, 5h. 45m. 3s. a.m.

| 10 | | | | | MAY, 1942. | | | | [RAPHAEL'S | | |
|---|---|---|---|---|---|---|---|---|---|---|---|
| D M | Neptune. Lat. | Neptune. Dec. | Herschel. Lat. | Herschel. Dec. | Saturn. Lat. | Saturn. Dec. | Jupiter. Lat. | Jupiter. Dec. | Mars. Lat. | Mars. Declin. | Mars. Declin. |
| | ° ′ | ° ′ | ° ′ | ° ′ | ° ′ | ° ′ | ° ′ | ° ′ | ° ′ | ° ′ | ° ′ |
| 1 | 1 N 21 | 2 N 15 | 0 S 11 | 19 N 49 | 1 S 47 | 18 N 13 | 0 S 13 | 22 N 57 | 1 N 25 | 24 N 50 | 24 N 49 |
| 3 | 1 21 | 2 15 | 0 11 | 19 51 | 1 46 | 18 17 | 0 13 | 22 58 | 1 25 | 24 47 | 24 46 |
| 5 | 1 21 | 2 16 | 0 11 | 19 52 | 1 46 | 18 20 | 0 13 | 23 0 | 1 25 | 24 44 | 24 43 |
| 7 | 1 21 | 2 17 | 0 11 | 19 54 | 1 46 | 18 24 | 0 13 | 23 2 | 1 25 | 24 41 | 24 39 |
| 9 | 1 20 | 2 18 | 0 10 | 19 55 | 1 46 | 18 27 | 0 12 | 23 3 | 1 24 | 24 36 | 24 34 |
| 11 | 1 20 | 2 18 | 0 10 | 19 57 | 1 46 | 18 30 | 0 12 | 23 5 | 1 24 | 24 31 | 24 28 |
| 13 | 1 20 | 2 19 | 0 10 | 19 58 | 1 46 | 18 34 | 0 12 | 23 6 | 1 24 | 24 25 | 24 22 |
| 15 | 1 20 | 2 19 | 0 10 | 20 0 | 1 45 | 18 37 | 0 12 | 23 8 | 1 24 | 24 19 | 24 15 |
| 17 | 1 20 | 2 20 | 0 10 | 20 1 | 1 45 | 18 40 | 0 12 | 23 9 | 1 23 | 24 12 | 24 8 |
| 19 | 1 20 | 2 20 | 0 10 | 20 2 | 1 45 | 18 44 | 0 11 | 23 10 | 1 23 | 24 4 | 24 0 |
| 21 | 1 20 | 2 21 | 0 10 | 20 4 | 1 45 | 18 47 | 0 11 | 23 11 | 1 23 | 23 55 | 23 51 |
| 23 | 1 20 | 2 21 | 0 10 | 20 5 | 1 45 | 18 50 | 0 11 | 23 12 | 1 22 | 23 46 | 23 41 |
| 25 | 1 20 | 2 22 | 0 10 | 20 7 | 1 45 | 18 53 | 0 11 | 23 13 | 1 22 | 23 36 | 23 31 |
| 27 | 1 20 | 2 22 | 0 10 | 20 8 | 1 45 | 18 56 | 0 10 | 23 14 | 1 22 | 23 26 | 23 20 |
| 29 | 1 20 | 2 22 | 0 10 | 20 10 | 1 45 | 18 59 | 0 10 | 23 15 | 1 21 | 23 15 | 23 9 |
| 31 | 1 20 | 2 22 | 0 10 | 20 11 | 1 44 | 19 2 | 0 10 | 23 16 | 1 21 | 23 3 | |

| D M | D W | Sidereal Time. | ☉ Long. | ☉ Dec. | ☽ Long. | ☽ Lat. | ☽ Dec. | MIDNIGHT. ☽ Long. | MIDNIGHT. ☽ Dec. |
|---|---|---|---|---|---|---|---|---|---|
| | | H. M. S. | ° ′ ″ | ° ′ | ° ′ ″ | ° ′ | ° ′ | ° ′ ″ | ° ′ |
| 1 | F | 2 35 8 | 10 ♉ 28 23 | 14 N 58 | 18 ♏ 39 39 | 4 N 40 | 12 S 53 | 26 ♏ 11 46 | 14 S 33 |
| 2 | S | 2 39 4 | 11 26 34 | 15 16 | 3 ♐ 44 35 | 5 1 | 15 58 | 11 ♐ 16 50 | 17 7 |
| 3 | 𝕾 | 2 43 1 | 12 24 44 | 15 34 | 18 47 18 | 5 2 | 17 58 | 26 14 54 | 18 30 |
| 4 | M | 2 46 58 | 13 22 52 | 15 52 | 3 ♑ 38 41 | 4 42 | 18 42 | 10 ♑ 57 52 | 18 36 |
| 5 | Tu | 2 50 54 | 14 20 59 | 16 9 | 18 11 50 | 4 3 | 18 11 | 25 20 14 | 17 29 |
| 6 | W | 2 54 51 | 15 19 4 | 16 26 | 2 ♒ 22 49 | 3 11 | 16 32 | 9 ♒ 19 33 | 15 20 |
| 7 | Th | 2 58 47 | 16 17 8 | 16 43 | 16 10 31 | 2 9 | 13 56 | 22 55 54 | 12 22 |
| 8 | F | 3 2 44 | 17 15 11 | 16 59 | 29 35 59 | 1 1 | 10 40 | 6 ♓ 11 6 | 8 50 |
| 9 | S | 3 6 40 | 18 13 12 | 17 16 | 12 ♓ 41 38 | 0 S 8 | 6 55 | 19 7 57 | 4 57 |
| 10 | 𝕾 | 3 10 37 | 19 11 12 | 17 32 | 25 30 28 | 1 16 | 2 57 | 1 ♈ 49 32 | 0 55 |
| 11 | M | 3 14 33 | 20 9 11 | 17 47 | 8 ♈ 5 30 | 2 18 | 1 N 6 | 14 18 41 | 3 N 5 |
| 12 | Tu | 3 18 30 | 21 7 8 | 18 3 | 20 29 22 | 3 13 | 5 2 | 26 37 48 | 6 54 |
| 13 | W | 3 22 27 | 22 5 4 | 18 18 | 2 ♉ 44 13 | 3 58 | 8 42 | 8 ♉ 48 48 | 10 24 |
| 14 | Th | 3 26 23 | 23 2 58 | 18 32 | 14 51 42 | 4 31 | 11 58 | 20 53 5 | 13 25 |
| 15 | F | 3 30 20 | 24 0 51 | 18 47 | 26 53 6 | 4 52 | 14 43 | 2 ♊ 51 53 | 15 52 |
| 16 | S | 3 34 16 | 24 58 42 | 19 1 | 8 ♊ 49 35 | 5 1 | 16 50 | 14 46 23 | 17 37 |
| 17 | 𝕾 | 3 38 13 | 25 56 32 | 19 15 | 20 42 29 | 4 56 | 18 12 | 26 38 6 | 18 36 |
| 18 | M | 3 42 9 | 26 54 21 | 19 28 | 2 ♋ 33 30 | 4 38 | 18 47 | 8 ♋ 28 59 | 18 47 |
| 19 | Tu | 3 46 6 | 27 52 8 | 19 41 | 14 24 56 | 4 8 | 18 33 | 20 21 43 | 18 8 |
| 20 | W | 3 50 2 | 28 49 54 | 19 54 | 26 19 48 | 3 27 | 17 30 | 2 ♌ 19 40 | 16 40 |
| 21 | Th | 3 53 59 | 29 47 37 | 20 7 | 8 ♌ 21 50 | 2 37 | 15 39 | 14 26 54 | 14 27 |
| 22 | F | 3 57 56 | 0 ♊ 45 19 | 20 19 | 20 35 27 | 1 38 | 13 5 | 26 48 6 | 11 32 |
| 23 | S | 4 1 52 | 1 43 0 | 20 31 | 3 ♍ 5 27 | 0 34 | 9 51 | 9 ♍ 28 9 | 8 1 |
| 24 | 𝕾 | 4 5 49 | 2 40 39 | 20 42 | 15 56 46 | 0 N 34 | 6 4 | 22 31 50 | 4 1 |
| 25 | M | 4 9 45 | 3 38 17 | 20 53 | 29 13 48 | 1 42 | 1 52 | 6 ♎ 3 0 | 0 S 20 |
| 26 | Tu | 4 13 42 | 4 35 53 | 21 4 | 12 ♎ 59 40 | 2 47 | 2 S 34 | 20 3 48 | 4 48 |
| 27 | W | 4 17 38 | 5 33 27 | 21 14 | 27 15 16 | 3 44 | 7 1 | 4 ♏ 33 40 | 9 9 |
| 28 | Th | 4 21 35 | 6 31 1 | 21 24 | 11 ♏ 58 22 | 4 28 | 11 11 | 19 28 32 | 13 3 |
| 29 | F | 4 25 31 | 7 28 33 | 21 34 | 27 3 4 | 4 54 | 14 44 | 4 ♐ 40 44 | 16 10 |
| 30 | S | 4 29 28 | 8 26 4 | 21 43 | 12 ♐ 20 6 | 5 0 | 17 19 | 19 59 45 | 18 10 |
| 31 | 𝕾 | 4 33 25 | 9 23 34 | 21 52 | 27 38 13 | 4 44 | 18 41 | 5 ♑ 14 5 | 18 52 |

First Quarter—May 23, 9h. 10m. 37s. a.m.

**Full Moon—May 30, 5h. 28m. 53s. a.m.**

*EPHEMERIS*] **MAY, 1942.** 11

| D M | Venus. Lat. | Venus. Declin. | | Mercury. Lat. | Mercury. Declin. | | ☽ ☊ Node. |
|---|---|---|---|---|---|---|---|
| | ° ′ | ° ′ | ° ′ | ° ′ | ° ′ | ° ′ | ° ′ |
| 1 | 0 S 56 | 2 S 49 | | 1 N 23 | 19 N 51 | | 10 ♍ 28 |
| | | | 2 S 27 | | | 20 N 30 | |
| 3 | 1 4 | 2 6 | | 1 41 | 21 6 | | 10 21 |
| | | | 1 44 | | | 21 39 | |
| 5 | 1 12 | 1 21 | | 1 56 | 22 10 | | 10 15 |
| | | | 0 59 | | | 22 38 | |
| 7 | 1 19 | 0 36 | | 2 8 | 23 4 | | 10 9 |
| | | | 0 13 | | | 23 28 | |
| 9 | 1 26 | 0 N 9 | | 2 17 | 23 48 | | 10 2 |
| | | | 0 N 33 | | | 24 7 | |
| 11 | 1 32 | 0 56 | | 2 24 | 24 23 | | 9 56 |
| | | | 1 19 | | | 24 37 | |
| 13 | 1 38 | 1 43 | | 2 26 | 24 49 | | 9 50 |
| | | | 2 6 | | | 24 58 | |
| 15 | 1 43 | 2 30 | | 2 26 | 25 5 | | 9 43 |
| | | | 2 54 | | | 25 11 | |
| 17 | 1 48 | 3 18 | | 2 21 | 25 14 | | 9 37 |
| | | | 3 41 | | | 25 16 | |
| 19 | 1 52 | 4 5 | | 2 12 | 25 16 | | 9 31 |
| | | | 4 29 | | | 25 14 | |
| 21 | 1 56 | 4 53 | | 2 0 | 25 11 | | 9 24 |
| | | | 5 17 | | | 25 6 | |
| 23 | 1 59 | 5 41 | | 1 44 | 25 0 | | 9 18 |
| | | | 6 5 | | | 24 53 | |
| 25 | 2 2 | 6 29 | | 1 25 | 24 44 | | 9 12 |
| | | | 6 53 | | | 24 34 | |
| 27 | 2 4 | 7 17 | | 1 2 | 24 22 | | 9 5 |
| | | | 7 41 | | | 24 10 | |
| 29 | 2 6 | 8 5 | | 0 34 | 23 57 | | 8 59 |
| | | | 8 28 | | | 23 43 | |
| 31 | 2 7 | 8 52 | | 0 5 | 23 27 | | 8 52 |

**Mutual Aspects.**

1. ☿ P ♅.
2. ♂ ⊻ ♇. [PΨ. ♄ ☌ ♅.
3. ☉ Q Ψ. ☿ ✱ ♀, △ Ψ. ♀ ☍ &
4. ☿ ⊥ ♂, ☌ ♄, ☌ ♅.
5. ☉ ∠ ♀. ♀ ✱ ♄, ✱ ♅.
[♂ ⊥ ♄, ⊥ ♅.
7. ☉ ⊥ ♃. ☿ P ♃, ✱ ♇.
9. ☿ P ♇. ♀ △ ♇.
10. ☿ ⊻ ♂.
11. ☿ P ♂.
13. ☉ Q ♇.
14. ☉ P ♄.
15. ☉ ⊻ ♃. ♀ P Ψ.
17. ♀ Q ♃.
18. ☉ △ Ψ. ☿ ∠ ♇. ♀ □ ♂.
19. ♀ ∠ ♅.
21. ☉ P ♅, ♀ ∠ ♄. ♂ ∠ ♅, Q Ψ.
22. ☉ ☌ ♅. ♂ P ♇.
23. ☉ ∠ ♂, ☌ ♄. ♂ ∠ ♄.
25. ☉ ✱ ♇.
28. ☿ ✱ ♀. ♀ ⊥ ♅. ♃ □ Ψ.
29. ☿ P ♇. ♂ P ♃.
30. ♀ ✱ ♃, ⊥ ♄. ∇ Ψ.

| D M | Ψ Long. | ♅ Long. | ♄ Long. | ♃ Long. | ♂ Long. | ♀ Long. | ☿ Long. | ☉ | ♇ | Ψ | ♅ | ♄ | ♃ | ♂ | ♀ | ☿ |
|---|---|---|---|---|---|---|---|---|---|---|---|---|---|---|---|---|
| | ° ′ | ° ′ | ° ′ | ° ′ | ° ′ | ° ′ | ° ′ | | | | | | | | | |
| 1 | 27 ♍ 28 | 29 ♉ 13 | 29 ♉ 5 | 21 ♊ 23 | 3 ♋ 12 | 25 ♓ 4 | 22 ♉ 58 | | | ∠ | | | | Q | △ | ☍ |
| 2 | 27 ℞ 26 | 29 17 | 29 12 | 21 35 | 3 49 | 26 8 | 24 56 | | △ | ✱ | ☍ | ☍ | | | | |
| S | 27 25 | 29 20 | 29 20 | 21 47 | 4 25 | 27 12 | 26 52 | | Q | | | | ☍ | | | |
| 4 | 27 24 | 29 24 | 29 28 | 21 59 | 5 2 | 28 17 | 28 44 | Q | | □ | | | | ☍ | □ | |
| 5 | 27 23 | 29 27 | 29 35 | 22 11 | 5 39 | 29 21 | 0 ♊ 34 | △ | | | Q | Q | | | | Q |
| 6 | 27 22 | 29 30 | 29 43 | 22 24 | 6 15 | 0 ♈ 26 | 2 21 | | ☍ | △ | △ | △ | Q | | ✱ | △ |
| 7 | 27 21 | 29 34 | 29 50 | 22 36 | 6 52 | 1 31 | 4 4 | □ | | Q | | | △ | Q | ∠ | |
| 8 | 27 20 | 29 37 | 29 58 | 22 48 | 7 29 | 2 37 | 5 44 | | | | □ | □ | | | ⊻ | |
| 9 | 27 19 | 29 41 | 0 ♊ 6 | 23 1 | 8 5 | 3 42 | 7 21 | ✱ | Q | | | | | △ | | □ |
| S | 27 18 | 29 44 | 0 13 | 23 13 | 8 42 | 4 48 | 8 54 | | | ☍ | ✱ | ✱ | □ | | | |
| 11 | 27 18 | 29 48 | 0 21 | 23 26 | 9 19 | 5 53 | 10 23 | ∠ | △ | | | | | □ | ● | ✱ |
| 12 | 27 17 | 29 51 | 0 29 | 23 38 | 9 55 | 6 59 | 11 48 | ⊻ | | | ∠ | ∠ | ✱ | | | |
| 13 | 27 16 | 29 55 | 0 36 | 23 51 | 10 32 | 8 5 | 13 10 | | □ | | ⊻ | ⊻ | | | ⊻ | ∠ |
| 14 | 27 15 | 29 58 | 0 44 | 24 4 | 11 9 | 9 12 | 14 27 | | | Q | | | ∠ | ✱ | | ⊻ |
| 15 | 27 14 | 0 ♊ 2 | 0 52 | 24 17 | 11 46 | 10 18 | 15 41 | ☌ | | △ | ☌ | ☌ | ⊻ | ∠ | ∠ | |
| 16 | 27 14 | 0 5 | 1 0 | 24 29 | 12 23 | 11 24 | 16 51 | | ✱ | | | | | ⊻ | ✱ | |
| S | 27 13 | 0 9 | 1 7 | 24 42 | 12 59 | 12 31 | 17 57 | ⊻ | ∠ | | | | ☌ | | | ☌ |
| 18 | 27 12 | 0 12 | 1 15 | 24 55 | 13 36 | 13 38 | 18 59 | | ⊻ | □ | ⊻ | ⊻ | | | | |
| 19 | 27 12 | 0 16 | 1 23 | 25 8 | 14 13 | 14 45 | 19 56 | ∠ | | | ∠ | ∠ | | ☌ | □ | |
| 20 | 27 11 | 0 19 | 1 31 | 25 21 | 14 50 | 15 52 | 20 49 | ✱ | | ✱ | ✱ | ✱ | ⊻ | | | ⊻ |
| 21 | 27 11 | 0 23 | 1 39 | 25 34 | 15 27 | 16 59 | 21 38 | | ☌ | ∠ | | | ∠ | | | ∠ |
| 22 | 27 10 | 0 26 | 1 46 | 25 47 | 16 3 | 18 6 | 22 23 | | | | | | ✱ | ⊻ | △ | ✱ |
| 23 | 27 10 | 0 30 | 1 54 | 26 0 | 16 40 | 19 14 | 23 3 | □ | ⊻ | ⊻ | □ | □ | | ∠ | Q | |
| S | 27 9 | 0 33 | 2 2 | 26 13 | 17 17 | 20 21 | 23 39 | | ∠ | | | | | ✱ | | |
| 25 | 27 9 | 0 37 | 2 10 | 26 27 | 17 54 | 21 29 | 24 10 | △ | ✱ | ● | △ | △ | □ | | | □ |
| 26 | 27 8 | 0 40 | 2 17 | 26 40 | 18 31 | 22 37 | 24 36 | | | | Q | Q | | □ | | |
| 27 | 27 8 | 0 44 | 2 25 | 26 53 | 19 8 | 23 44 | 24 58 | Q | □ | ⊻ | | | △ | | ☍ | △ |
| 28 | 27 7 | 0 47 | 2 33 | 27 6 | 19 45 | 24 52 | 25 15 | | | ∠ | | | Q | | | Q |
| 29 | 27 7 | 0 51 | 2 41 | 27 20 | 20 21 | 26 0 | 25 28 | | △ | ✱ | ☍ | ☍ | | △ | | |
| 30 | 27 7 | 0 54 | 2 48 | 27 33 | 20 58 | 27 8 | 25 35 | ☍ | Q | | | | | Q | Q | |
| S | 27 7 | 0 58 | 2 56 | 27 46 | 21 35 | 28 17 | 25 38 | | | □ | | | ☍ | | △ | ☍ |

(The last nine columns, ☉ to ☿, are headed **Lunar Aspects.**)

**Last Quarter—May 7, 0h. 12m. 35s. p.m.**

Tokyo, Japan

May 15th, 1942
36 N 140 E

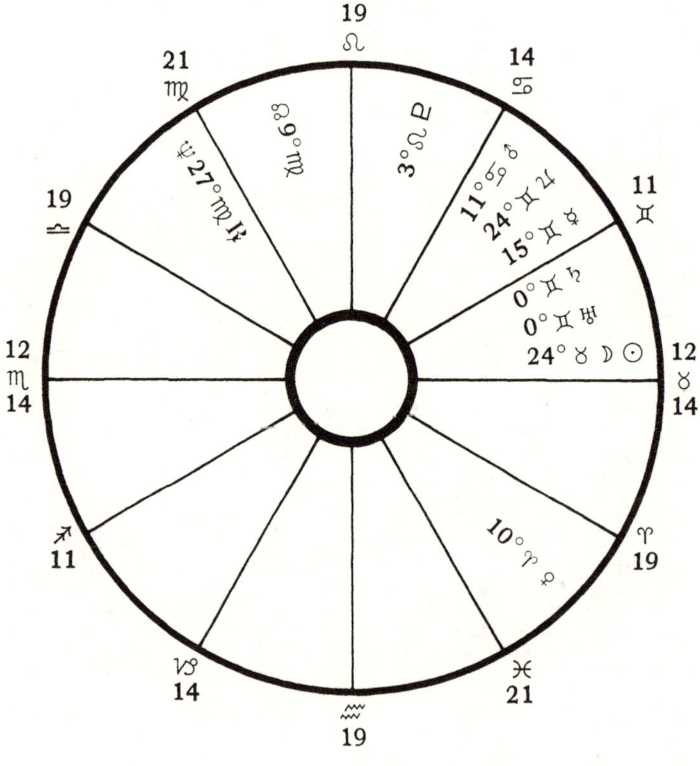


Most planets past MC and in decline; implies that several years of increasing problems soon will begin.

Leadership (10th) ruler in 7th reflects most attention to foreign affairs; attention to resources (4th), propaganda (3rd) and national morale (5th). Dictatorial policies (Pluto) past zenith but continues popular (trine Venus).

Berlin, Germany

May 15th, 1942
52 N 13 E

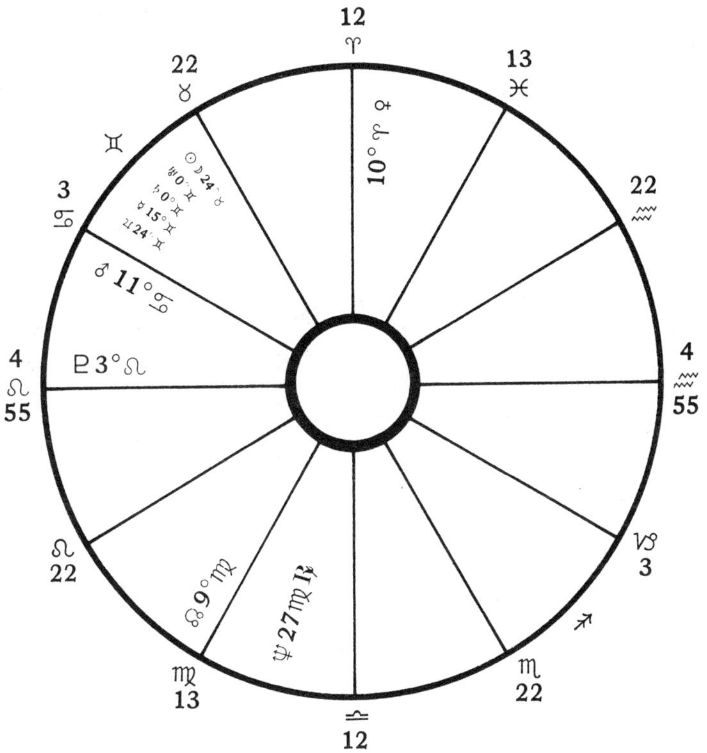


Pluto (dictatorship) on Asc (people) trine Venus at MC, marks probable peak of success and power, but the sequence may not be grasped quickly due to the concentration in the 11th house.

Neptune in 3rd (propaganda) fools the people successfully and they have a sense of well-being (Node in 2nd) (money).

Washington, D. C.

May 15th, 1942
39 N 77 W

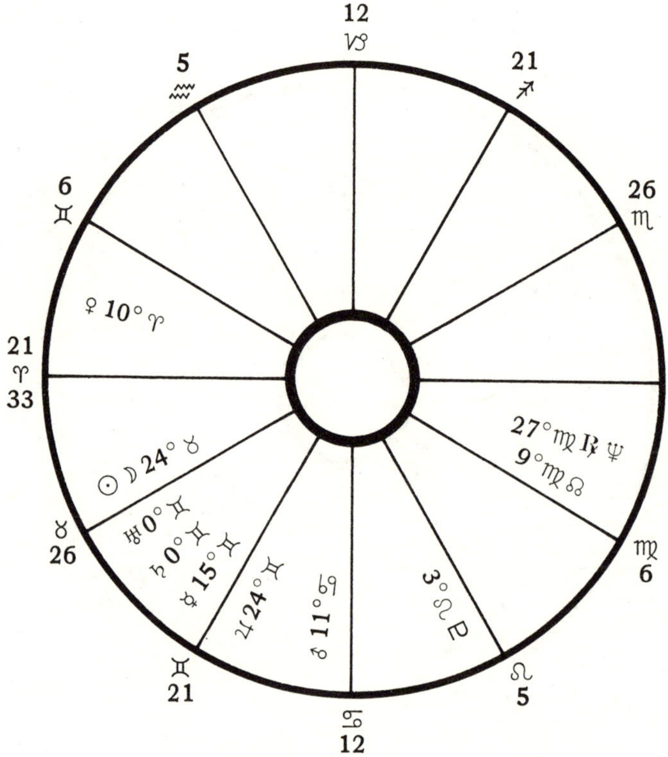


Most positions below horizon but rising; conjunction of Uranus Saturn; receding conjunction of Jupiter; Node exactly square 9° Gemini. Mars, ruler of Asc (the people) at cusp of 4th: a major low point. Major low in morale and values—a bullish index with Jupiter nearing 26° from Saturn.

London, England

May 15th, 1942
52 N 0 E

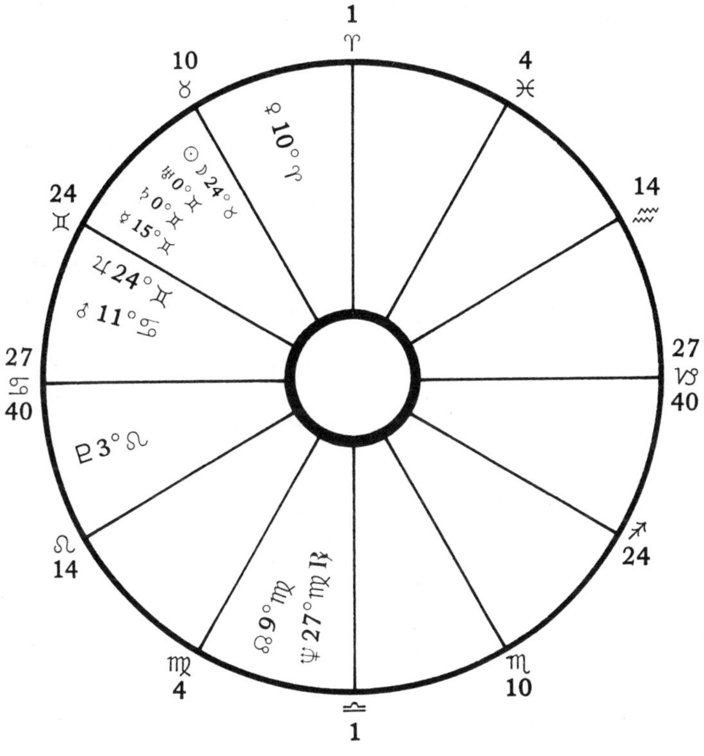


All positions at the East and rising; the heavy concentration in the 11th house reflects concentrated efforts in a dogged and aggressive national attitude (Mars rising in Asc (people) trine Venus near MC (love for leaders). Saturn Uranus conjunction reflects confidence and aid from 7th (foreign) and 8th (foreign resources).

Millions of dollars in manhours have been used to collect statistics, catalogue them and then run them through computers to try to define the cycles of business and its many facets. The result is a maze of data. There are the 41 to 43 month cycles, the 4½ year, 9 year, 10 years, 18 year or three times the 18 year for a 54 year affair. All of them are averages but acceptable by mathematical standards. For example, they locate several cycles of varying length which when averaged come to nine years although none of the cycles were precisely nine years duration but anywhere between perhaps 7 and 12 years long. So 9 years becomes a measure and the thing never meets anticipations. Back to collecting data they go. The real core is apparent in the cycle of the Node.

But to get back to our May 1942 Washington figure. Here we have a beautiful low point for conclusions on which to make some market estimates. First, there are major signs of a low ebb in national confidence and prospects of a revival. Prices are much depressed and what might be termed over-sold. But the action of the Node is the lead-off. After the square from Virgo to 9° of Gemini there is nothing until 1946 to halt an uptrend. Additional evidence is as follows.

Adverse or negative aspects between Jupiter, Saturn and Uranus depress, in one form or another, business activity and markets. A conjunction involving Saturn is notably severe. Such an event occurred when Jupiter was conjunct Saturn early in 1941 and then the Saturn Uranus conjunction in 1942. Relief from these depressing factors began to wane (angle relationships widened) as soon as the conjunctions became completed. Late in May 1942 Jupiter was approaching 26° away from Saturn, a bullish index, with little of bearish importance until 90° difference between Jupiter and Saturn appears. It occurs May 5th, 1946, which approximates the high in markets since 1942. From early 1946, factors were sustaining but not bullish until 1949, etc.

We could proceed and get into Ingress and Lunation charts, the part of Parallels and the details of interpretive method. It would soon tangle our goal of a perspective of market estimates. In our "over-simplified" method of cycle interpretation we keep everything as simple as possible and confine it to the following:

First, scanning the ephemeris positions for the period involved to note the interaction of Uranus, Saturn, Jupiter and the Node. Then we translate the positions into Sign-House and House-Sign notes. We can stop there and record when interaction occurs at critical angles of favorable and unfavorable aspects. (Favorable are those in the triology; unfavorable in the quadrature as already detailed). Then a trend prospect can be concluded.

Like statistical cycles reported these days about business, all agree they exist but the timing is something else. Every week in astro-cycles differs from any other week in history. Each week, each month and each year has to be plotted by itself. One thing that pushes the statistician up the wall is the apparent 'retrograde' pattern of a planet; it seems to go backward in its course and then go forward again. Sure, Jupiter makes its complete cycle in 12 years but one year it seems to bounce back and forth and then suddenly it goes ahead on course. In most cases a planet in retrograde has a reduced potency; the things it signifies seem to stick to routine.

It really does not disturb the situation except we simply are unable to can it, or tape or simplify the rules for cold storage use. We become like the chap who asked a world famous physician why, after all the expensive tests undeniably proved that a certain patient could not survive more than a few weeks the patient was alive and apparently vigorous after ten years. The physician is supposed to have replied: "Let's give thanks for what we know and not be over-disturbed over what we do not know."

As familiarity with these factors emerges and facility in their use develops the goals of confidence and profits will follow. It may be a cliche but 'knowledge is power' and in terms of markets, whether stocks, bonds or commodities, knowledge can be profits, security and peace of mind.

CHAPTER THIRTEEN

# PLANETARY ASPECTS OR ANGULAR RELATIONSHIPS

For ease of interpretation the solar system is charted in a 360° circle divided into 12 sections called houses with the noon position the Midheaven and 10th house segment, and eastern (left) horizon the ascendant and the 1st house.

The angles or aspects between planets are divided into numerous divisions but in general the most useful are the fourths or squares, the triology or trines and the fifths or quintiles. The squares in general are classed as bearish, unfavorable and activating. The trines are bullish, favorable, serene, constructive and the expansion urge.

The fifths or quintiles are generally ignored, but in mundane work covering markets and economic affairs they are very significant. Trend reversals usually are lost in the trine and the squares but are timed by the fifths. At the right a 360° circle has five divisions of 72° each. Visualize also 10 divisions of 36° each and 20 divisions of 18° each; all useful.

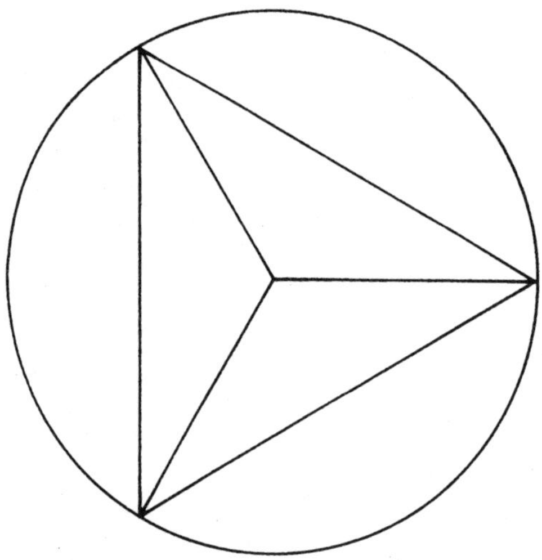

Often, to keep data clarified, it is well to consider waxing and waning aspects; as the angular relationship narrows it is waxing; as it widens it is waning. For example a waxing trine is labeled 120° while a waning trine is labeled 240°.

Keep in mind the square group of aspects, the 22½°, the 45°, 90°, 135°, 180°. The trines relate to 15°, 30°, 60°, 120°, etc, but note 135° relates to 45° also. Apparent contradiction is adjusted by noting the

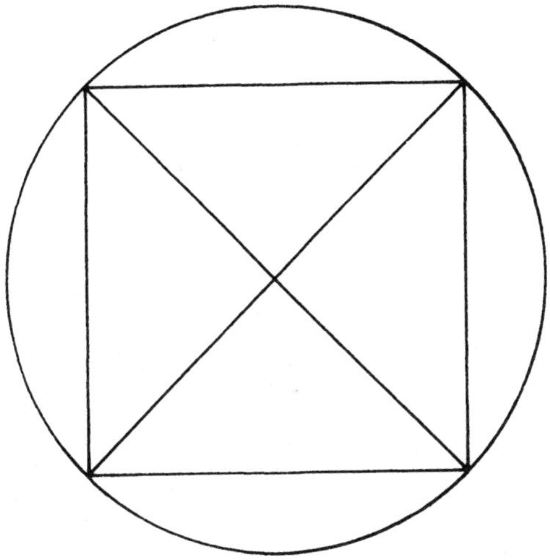

nature of the planets involved; a benefic such as Jupiter and Venus would have an aspect of the bullish tendencies.

The fifths or quintiles relate to 18°, 36°, 54°, 72°, etc. But quintiles often are turning or resolving areas. An upward market trend marked by a trine aspect situation which is waning comes to a quintile aspect

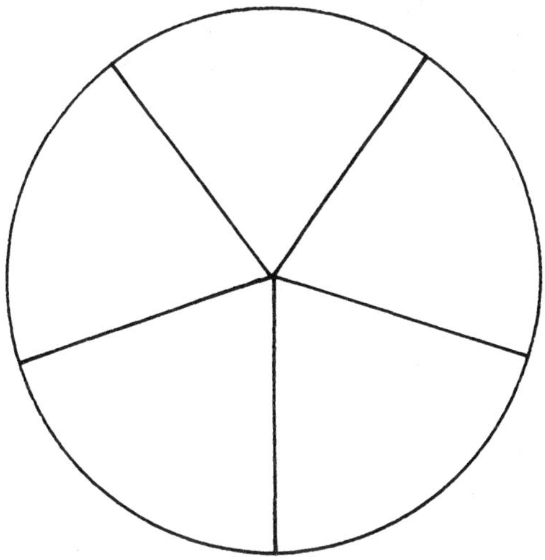

(the trine changes to quintile) and a decline appears; if followed by a waxing square type of aspect declining or bearish trends are confirmed.

The rule continues to keep it simple; in general stay with the potent aspects of the three groups and avoid trying to include every minor aspect.

CHAPTER FOURTEEN

# FORMATION OF A MARKET FORECAST

In the preceding chapter we attempted to work into a perspective of prevailing moods, opinions and circumstances dominant in a country at a specific time. By expanding the data we should be able to uncover something tangible to form some estimates of market trend probabilities.

The "over"-simplified method of planetary houses and sign-houses is expanded slightly by placing the positions in a locality chart or figure. As an initial example one day is examined for its local reaction in three widely separated localities, viz, Kansas City, New York City and the Philippines. (See the charts and comments on the next page).

To follow, the next example presents six charts set up for crucial market points from 1956 to 1970 inclusive. Notes appended each chart, if examined with bar charts of the stock market, such as the Industrials, for these years discussed, will aid in grasping the relationships.

Let us briefly recapitulate the step by step program of defining astro-cycles and then applying them as a basis of interpretation in estimating probable speculative market trends.

(A) We become familiar with planets in their natural house-signs and then sign-houses (see charts pages 59 and 60).

(B) The zodiac is divided into 12 divisions or houses and we become familiar with each house meaning (page 39).

(C) Geographical locality computing is learned (the complications of Ingresses, lunations, etc, are avoided).

(D) We synthesize planets in house locations and use sign rulership (see page 59) as in Horary methods for general estimates of a chart.

(E) Then natural house signs, plus sign-house interpretation, are added to consideration of rulerships and the planetary powers for detailed data.

(F) Keep in mind specific angular relationships of Jupiter, Saturn and Uranus are the key to stocks in the plus or minus, bullish or bearish, critical degrees noted in the text. Each commodity has its own combination of one or two of the foregoing plus either Mercury, or Venus, or Mars.

*August 18th, 1976.* The planetary positions are for Noon GMT from Raphael's Ephemeris for 1976. A Table of Houses (readily available is published by The Rosicrucian Fellowship, Oceanside, California, 318 pp. $4.50, for Latitude 1 to 66 degrees) gives the house cusps. From the Locality Maps on pages 8 and 9 and the latitude and longitude of each location compute the 10th House (MC) figure according to the directions on page 7.

It is suggested that a series of dates are selected, such as major highs and lows of markets, and charts like these set up. It will develop facility in interpretation. For stocks use New York; for wheat, corn, etc, use Chicago, etc. Primary attention should be directed to Uranus, Saturn and Jupiter.

New York, N. Y.

---

41 N 71 W
August 18th, 1976

---

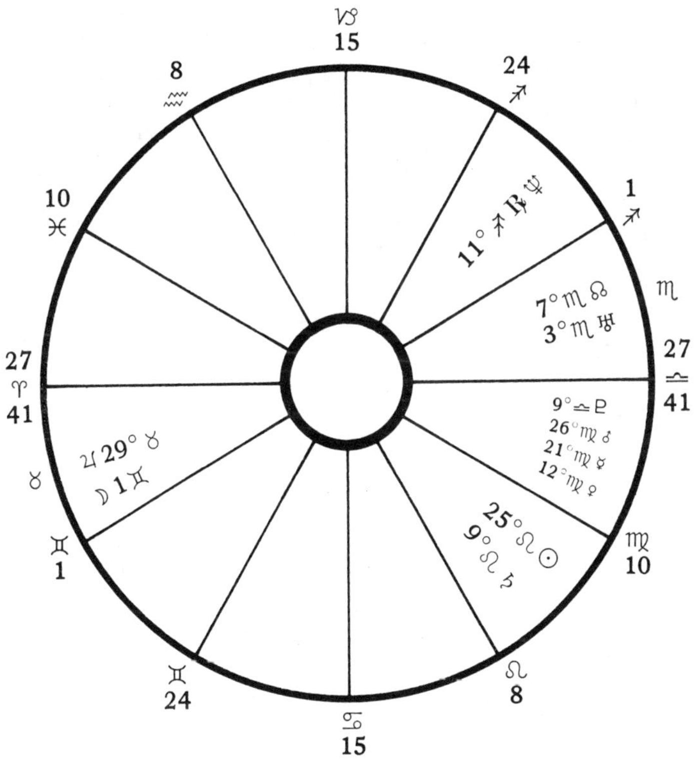


Outlook for stock market after Reblican Nat'l Convention today.

Uranus square Saturn (ruling the 10 and 11th) reflects doubts over business outlook. Saturn and Jupiter, with Jupiter now out of Gemini into Taurus, approach 72° which is a bearish point.

Stocks are bearish.

Kansas City, Mo.

39 N 95 W
August 18th, 1976

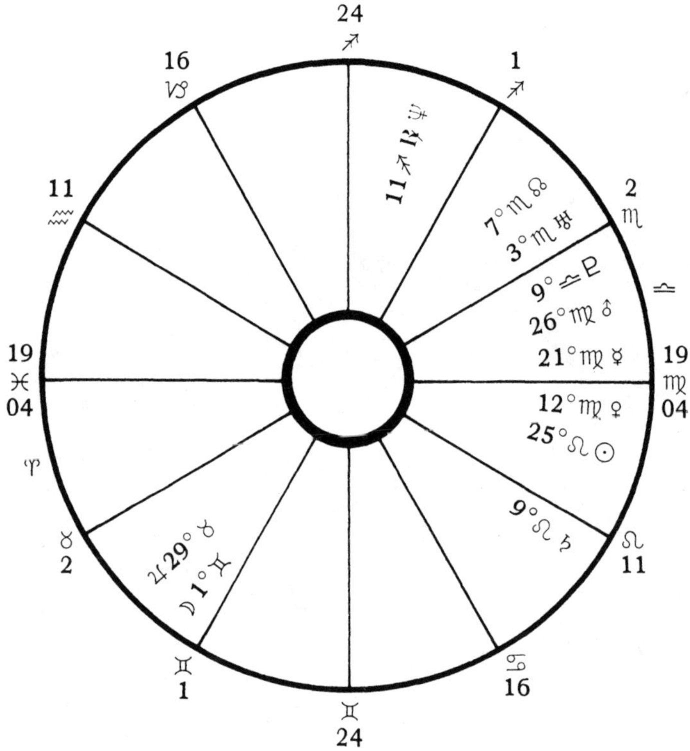


Nomination of a Republican for President. Unusually successful money, publicity and entertainment affair for the locality (ruler of 10th in 2nd and Moon 2nd ruling 5th). Two planets on Desc. and two factions. Ruler of 11th (incumbent) trine Neptune in 9th retrograde ruling 1st (confused public situation).

South Mindanao, Philippines

7 N 124 E
August 18th, 1976

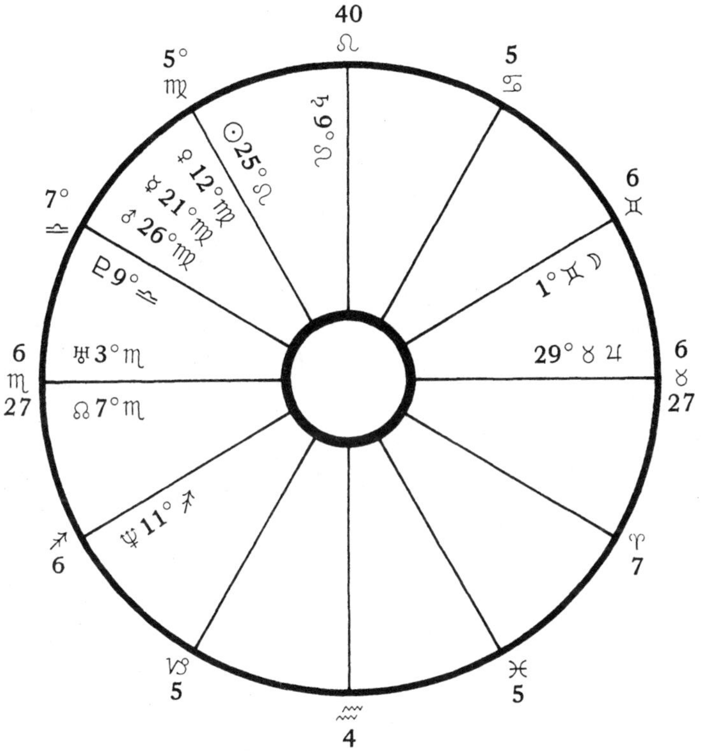


Same time as Nat'l Republican Convention; Earthquake and tidal wave with upwards of 20,000 homeless.

Uranus, ruler of 4th on Asc. square Saturn in 10th at MC which is square eclipse point of April 29th, 1976 on Descendant at 9° Taurus which is opposition Asc. and Uranus.

Here are some examples for study. Check with a market chart of stocks for 75 years, for example. After the rise from a 1949 low the Averages reached 741 on the Industrials in 1962 and then declined to 525. Subsequently was a rise to 1001 late in 1965 and a decline in 1966 to 736.

In 1956, after a steep rise from 1953, the Industrials wavered at 524. In 1956 and 1957 they formed a triple high; thus the wavering cyclic figures of January and May 1956 which are appended.

But the factors prevented confusion over prospects and patiencc was the only need. It is the Node and the interaction (angles) between Jupiter and Saturn and then Uranus with both of them which gives us our basic keys. Keep it simple is the rule; rule breakers will not listen so they will tangle with Parallels, then add Venus, Mars and Mercury in the search for the absolutes which in reality do not exist.

New York City

41 N 74 W
January 15, 1956

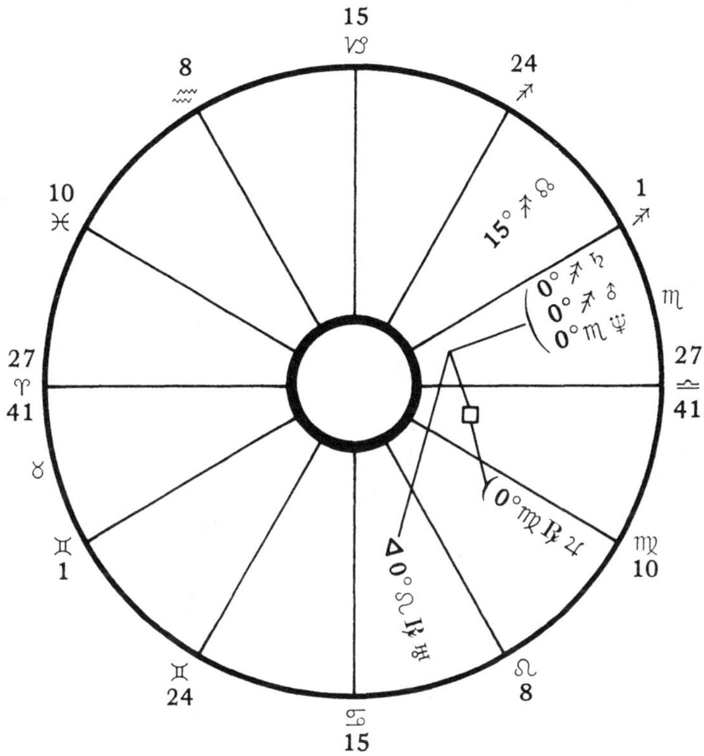


Here Saturn is square Jupiter—very bearish usually but here the square is brief and Jupiter is apparent retrograde weakening it.

Trine to Uranus also weak as Uranus is retrograde. Then the Node is not at a critical point. Indication: probable peak in the offing, but not now.

New York City

41 N 71 W
March 6th, 1962

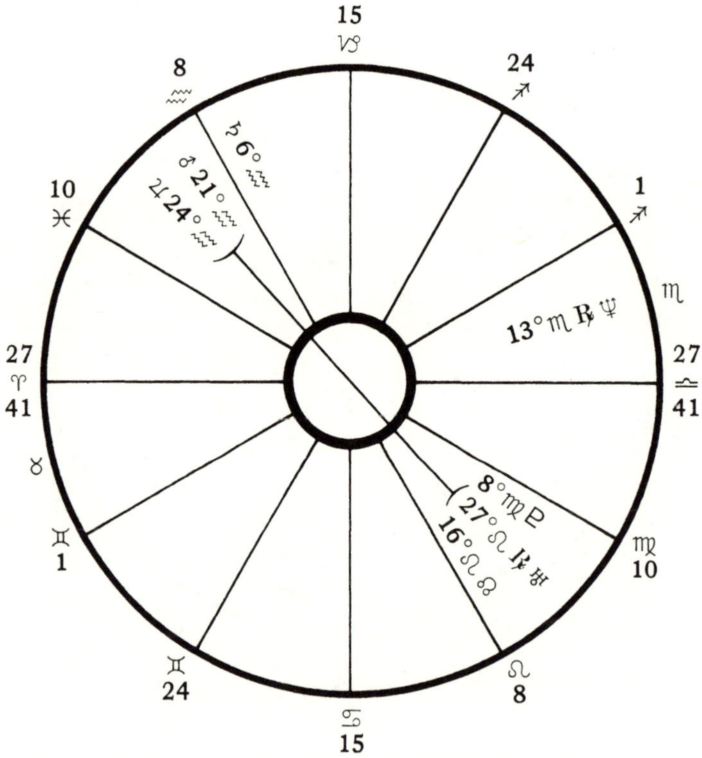


Bearish data first half of year with Jupiter Saturn at 18° (bearish) Mars conjunct Jupiter opposition Uranus. Pluto square the Gemini point 7°–9°. Downside initial objective Node sextile 9° Gemini in late July and then September Jupiter Saturn of bullish 27° point. Nothing significant to deter uptrend maturing until August 1965 with Node 9° Gemini.

New York City

41 N 71 W
May 1st, 1956

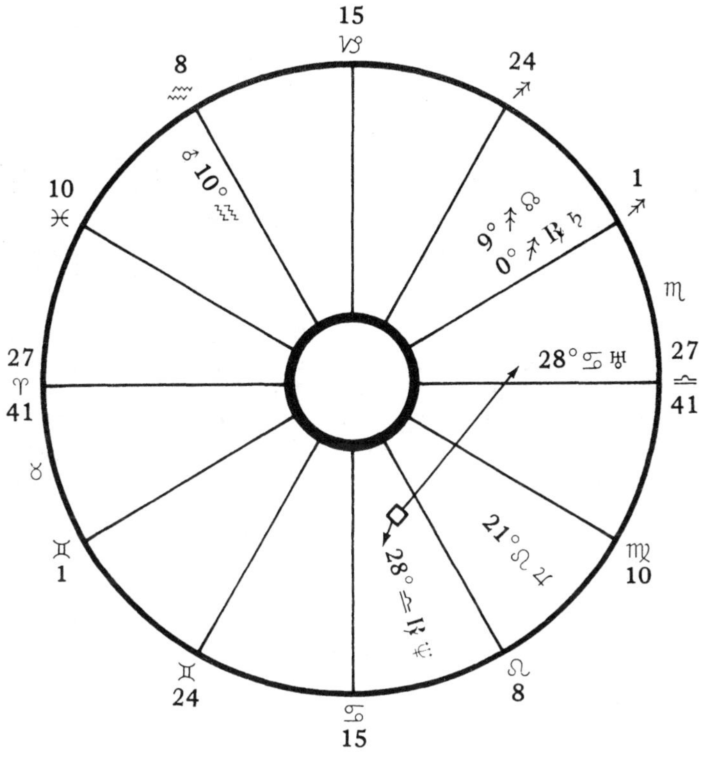

Node has reached opposition to 9° Gemini, a market top index.

Neptune square Uranus heavy distribution; confusion over 11th and 7th house public policies.

Nothing bullish. Look for downside confirmation at Jupiter-Saturn 72° point in mid-July. Probable low *November 1957* when Node reaches 150° to 9° Gemini point and September Jupiter Saturn sextile confirmed.

These examples of market trends from late in 1968 through 1971 indicate cyclic data was correct, and economic opinion, professional judgment and 'insider' confidence were all wrong. It was a classic rout of the conglomerate craze, the pyramiding of growth stocks, and bloody nosing the wonder kids and their new fresh-from-graduate-school economics.

Actually it was perhaps the sadest and ruinous time for the new generation of 'investors' convinced in the ease of a fast buck. In reality it was 1929 in collapsed situations again, but instead of the debt of margin calls which could not be met, this collapse erased the buying capital of thousands, but who hold their certificates today hoping the improbable will occur and they may "get even."

New York City

41 N 71 W
Nov 24th, 1968

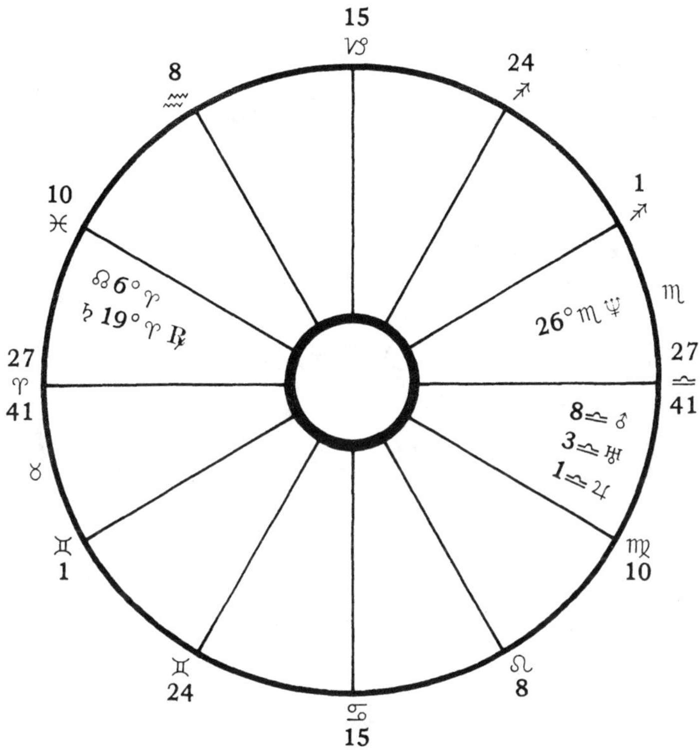


Transport Average has a new high but the Industrials failed by 6 points and technical weakness expands. Jupiter near conjunct Uranus with both opposed by Saturn, a major bearish index.

Saturn, ruling 10th, in the Asc., with Neptune ruling 12th in 7th—inherent decline of national confidence over leadership in foreign policies.

New York City

41 N 71 W
January 1st, 1970

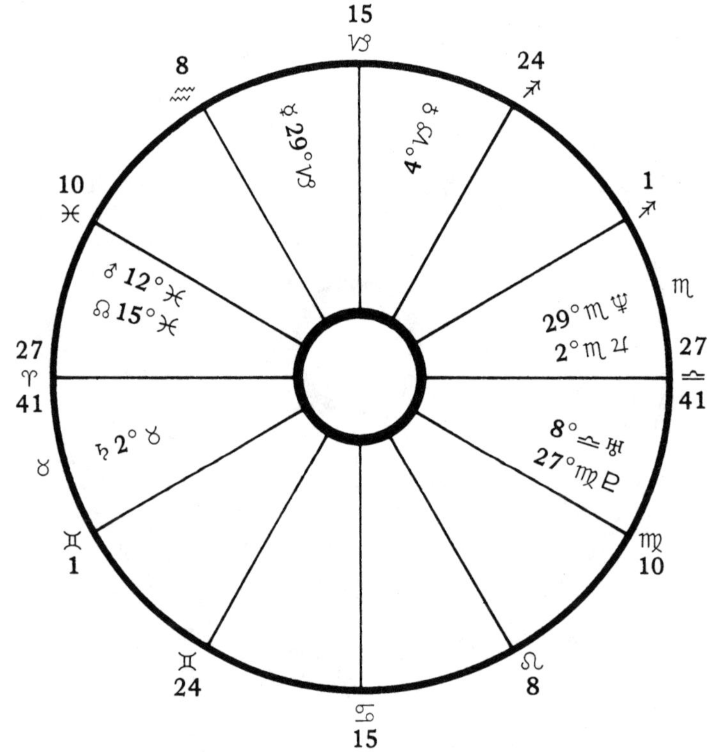


Sept 1969 rally under Jupiter-Saturn 150° now exhausted with bearish Jupiter–Saturn 180°—rejection of foreign affairs due to Jupiter in 7th ruling 8th and 9th, opposed by Saturn in 2nd (money) ruling 10th (leadership policies).

Technical structure very weak and nothing bullish until Node reaches 9° in late April 1970.

New York City

41 N 71 W
April 28th, 1970

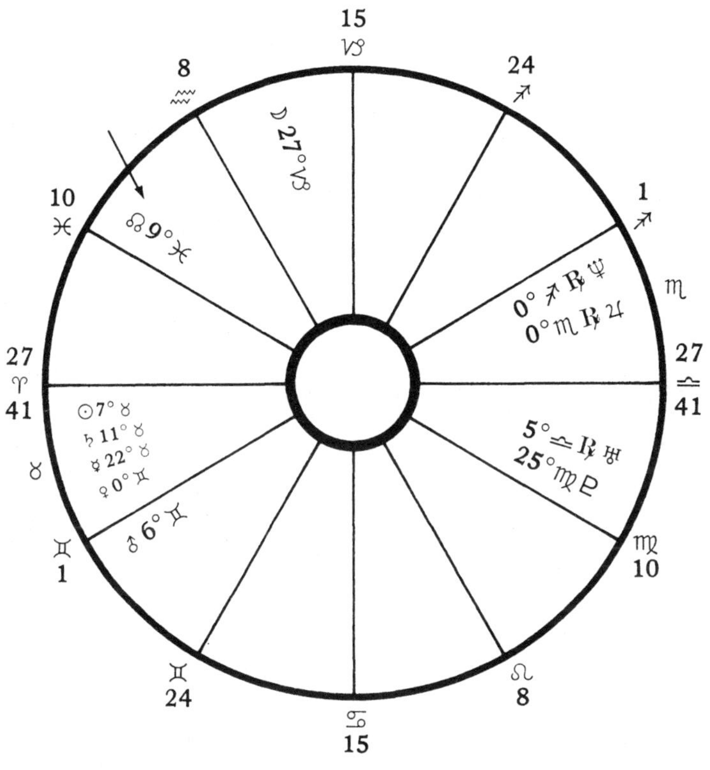

Node at 9° Pisces in square to Geminin 9° critical point; due is an important low. Industrials have declined 368 points, more than 30%, since late in 1968. Technical rebound would carry to March 24th, 1971 for 162° Jupiter Saturn with Jupiter stationery. Such a pattern would offer a low in early November 1971 with Node at 9° Aquarius, trine to Gemini 9°.

# Section III

# MARKET CHARTS

## A CORRELATION OF THE GEOMETRICAL METHOD

A simplified scientific procedure of charting the prices of grain and security markets. An aid in forecasting and co-ordinating price trends with cyclical and technical factors.

# FOREWORD

The charting fundamentals and their applications presented in this section originally were published by the author in the book "**MARKET CHARTS**—A Correlation of the Geometrical Method" copyright 1934, and for many years out of print. This new edition continues virtually unchanged except for an added number of working examples to illustrate workaday applications.

More than fifty years have elapsed since I first began to delve into possible clues to panics and booms plus the never-ending constant price changes in markets for stocks and commodities in particular. That study brought intensive research in the late 1920's and became professional advisory services until retirement in 1971. Advertising was never used as the clientele developed from readers of several national publications to which I was a regular contributor from 1933 to 1957 when I assumed full time effort as analyst for a Stock Exchange organization.

Intrusion of the biographical comment is to underscore that fifty years of market efforts which contained some forty years of first hand relations with people and organizations in markets produced experience. Again and again many of the finest people sought me out for suggestions in trading and investment procedure. Too many times market profits and their successful interpretation of market potentials had turned sour. In a few instances the lessons were accepted, studied and then, following the basic factors devoid of the 'fear and greed' emotions, success became realized.

Human perception is blunted when too many trees block a view of the forest. Tape watching, hanging over the news ticker, or carefully scrutinizing orders being written by a broker interspersed with shouts: "the floor is selling so-and-so," "Cargill is buying wheat," or "A big extra is about to be announced by such-and-such company," are suicidal. All a successful trader needs from a broker is confirmation of buying and selling orders, and refusal to let the broker say more than to give quotes in order to satisfy his feeling of continuing your good-will. Yes, stated bluntly, be student enough to make your decisions without any comment from anyone; if in doubt do not make the commitment.

The axiom is that a little knowledge can be a dangerous thing, which might be paraphrased to the concept that a little market success can make a dunce out of a potential investor. Often a person checks market fluctuations in newspapers, chart books or simply conversations with others. Daily ranges of prices become potential gold mines, or a 50% or more gain in the price of a stock over a period of weeks begins to form the might-have-been profit. With some extra funds available some ideas are gathered, or a 'hot-tip' is followed. Success in the form of a good profit accrues. Now is the time to jump in again, usually in a larger transaction. The project works nicely. But this time no grabbing a fair profit; 'inside' information says the commitment will double, or triple, or produce even greater gain. This person often hangs on too long; then a reaction develops. Instead of getting out, the promise to get out when a rally appears is substituted. The rally fails or falls short and profits are eroded until all the commitment is in loss. In a stock the result is a candidate for wall-paper; in a commodity the option expires and a sale is mandatory unless delivery is accepted which is something else.

Profitable speculation and investment in securities, or, in grain futures, is principally dependent on how comprehensive a grasp the operator has of the technical factors at work within the markets. All the luck in the world never took the place of astute technical knowledge, plus the ability to apply it. Without technical knowledge, in greater or lesser degree, the market operator is only a gambler naively "playing the market"; when, in consideration of the stakes involved, a small amount of study would enable him to become an intelligent speculator.

With minor exceptions, all markets operate under basic natural laws which govern supply and demand. A rhythmic ebb and flow is always perceptible in the movements of prices. It is by gauging this motion that the state of supply and demand is interpreted.

The purpose of this brochure is to present methods of interpreting the important technical factors operating in markets. The method of approach and the manner of application coincides, and is a part of, those ancient laws which form the foundation of modern science. They have not, to my knowledge, ever been applied in this somewhat unique manner to the charted movements of market prices. But, although the application may seem new and much of the method of co-ordination original, the entire foundation is as old as mathematics and philosophy.

At first inspection, the methods of procedure are likely to seem difficult to apply readily. Invariably this is the situation whenever a new subject is first approached. However, I am confident that with a little application anyone interested in markets will be gratified with the results encountered.

All those who are interested in markets, whether as a vocation, or avocation, cannot spend long periods of time, or invest considerable money, for extensive economic research and study. Therefore the economic specialist and the economic service organizations. An automobile owner need not be an expert mechanic simply because he drives his car; but, some knowledge of motor mechanics, together with a road map, contributes to the success of any journey. So it is with market operations: anyone with any market interests, large or small, always finds the relatively small time and trouble it takes to keep several market charts an investment that pays large profits in both money and a better sense of confidence. With greater confidence comes power and the initiative ability for decisive, profitable action.

In the majority of instances commodity commitments are shunned. When more money becomes available commitments in another stock or a variety of stocks occurs which becomes a 'portfolio' when in reality a mixed bunch of stocks are carried in Street name in an account. In the course of years some become 'winners' and others 'losers'; an avocation develops in a daily reading of the market page quotations.

Any person with the intention of finding a means of earning several thousands of dollars a year as self-employed, or as an avocation, makes careful preparation for the choice and then the operating know-how. The smallest sort of retailing operation requires many elements to become successful. The Small Business Administration, which often plans and assists new business formations, reports four out of five fail in five years. But emotionally anyone with interest in markets and a bit of money believes winning is inevitable. If there is one salient and primary fact to obey constantly, without the slightest deviation, and follow-through with patience, it is to:

> graph the statistics of market action according to the means of estimating time and price in daily and weekly price ranges. The geometrical rules presented in the text cannot be compromised at all. And adhere strictly to the market action revealed in the graphs, not rumors.

Years ago a long time client revealed he had been a floor trader on the Chicago Board of Trade for many years. Forced to retire due to health problems he requested an address change to reach him at a small village near Hudson's Bay in Northern Canada. A year or so later he reported intensive study of this graph method had intrigued him that he was experimenting with 5 M bushels, mailing orders to Chicago by regular mail, which sometimes took ten days for delivery. He said he felt he was groping in the dark but handled it by stop-loss orders selected from trend channels of the charts from the daily ranges picked up from several radio stations with market news broadcasts. It was a few years later he called on me to relate his losses, using the stops religiously, had been minimal, while some very handsome profits had been realized by acting on the potential swings and timing. This example leads me to suggest, as I have done many times:

> Invest your time in serious study and see you grasp how the application of mathematical elements exhibits market activity. Only then venture commitments and your capital, based only on conclusions drawn from your judgment.

You may feel these comments are rather presumptuous and naive enough to imply you do not know better. Frankly, more than forty years of experience have proven such reactions are a mistake. The more capital you may venture the greater the hazard if you cast them aside and ignore them.

Like a nautical chart aids the navigators at sea to maintain objectives and positions, market charts are of tremendous value in all market transactions. Market charts are a graphic statistical view of price movements in the market, sometimes from hour to hour, sometimes from day to day, week to week, month to month, and even a view of year to year.

The problem of market activity is, in the final practical analysis, that of prices. To profit we must buy lower than we sell. It is trite to point out that a $100 stock is a bargain if it is about to move higher, while a $2 stock is expensive if it is about to go down. But, most people realize the greatest urge to buy just before a high is reached. The reason for this psychology is obvious. But its basis lies in the lack of a grasp of much of the technical perspective of the market itself.

So much material has been published on the importance of the economic market charts during the last several years that market students no longer view charts lightly. Yet, of all the methods I have examined and used the geometrical approach is the only form that enables the student to co-ordinate the fundamental laws of supply and demand, the the element of time, the problem of resistance and objective and the basis of price, with the astro-economic cyclical factors.

I am particularly indebted to my partner, Mr George E. Liggett, for the basic practical application of the geometrical method to the problem of market trends. His first application of phases of the method was used in grain markets over a decade ago. These basic ideas were later amplified and expanded by our associate, Mr Virgil Moore, now deceased. Best known as The Moon Man in the grain markets, Virgil Moore's phenomenal forecasts will be long remembered. His interpretation of markets was based almost entirely on the various phases of the geometrical method of charting.

The material which follows warrants careful study. Each phase of the discussion is part of an ultimate whole. It is suggested:—that the material is first read through carefully, without any attempt to apply the principles laid down. Then a general perspective will be attained, which, on second reading, will afford a quicker grasp of every step. Then apply the method to a chart of current interest. With practice will come facility, and as facility develops the many combinations and possibilities of this method will be found.

CHAPTER ONE

# GEOMETRICAL FUNDAMENTALS

The increasing use of charts, as a concise visual record of the fluctuations of grain and security market prices, indicates their decided value in speculative and investment operations. Particularly since the crash in 1929, a comprehensive grasp of the technical factors operating within markets is recognized to be of importance, and in many ways supersede such items as company earnings, overhead, fixed charges, credit and indebtedness. Statistical items bear on problems of market prices, but markets boom and crash before such news is available. Market charts usually signal important changes. They are keys to the factors of supply and demand which operate in every market. Market technicalities, as registered on charts, take first place in all forms of market interpretation.

Over recent years, a great deal of material has been published on methods of charting market statistics. Much of the material is of great value; but, principally to illustrate the record of the past or to estimate current technical conditions. Very little of the material is of the slightest use in forecasting. But, as the means of "half a loaf" of observational material is better than none, so even a meager chart is better than none.

The idea that all markets operate according to the natural laws of supply and demand, in a rhythmic ebb and flow of price changes, is rather difficult to grasp at first glance. It is simpler to take the view that all prices are either "put up" or "pushed down" by several, or one, "insiders." But, like most half truths, such a premise simply distorts a true grasp of markets. Prices are and have been "rigged," but no "rigger" or pool met success bucking the general trend. Markets move in waves, ofttimes against the wishes of the majority or in spite of every human effort to reverse the trend. The explanation of this condition lies in those natural laws which are related, and are a part of, the cyclical movements of mass psychology.

It is in an examination of these natural cycles that both individual investors and speculators, and the managers of large funds can locate the key to the many inexplicable market trends. Anything that is as prosaic and practical as markets might appear to have little in common with ancient philosophy, but market trends are simply an exact reflection of the total hopes, fears and desires of great masses of people. Markets are a part of living and so is philosophy.

Lack of space prevents an examination of the philosophical and psychological backgrounds of markets. It is necessary, however, so as to clarify phases of the geometrical method of charting, to refer to some of the fundamental data.

Practically all modern "discoveries" are new applications, and new variations, of things which have gone before. The extraordinary developments in modern atomic and electronic science were bequeathed to us from ancient times. The observations of Thales of Miletus in about 600 B.C., the work of Democritus in Ancient Greece, and Leucretius in Ancient Rome, forms much basis for mathematical science in modern times. Euclid, the father of geometry, and Pythagoras, who is credited with raising mathematics to a science, presented tenets and observations which have never been refuted down through centuries of research and observation. Modern physics continues to view the principles of Democritus as basic. As Tyndall quotes them, they are the foundation of modern scientific thought. One principle is that "nothing happens by chance. Every occurrence has its cause from which it follows by necessity."

Kepler's doctrine of the concurrence of parallels at a single point at infinity, and his principle of continuity in relation to the infinitely great, relates to all geometrical figures. This thesis, as applied to natural law, was amplified by Descartes and Newton. There is no reason why charts of market statistics, if drawn according to geometrical design, cannot be another application of these premises.

A Pythagorean proposition is that all things consist of three—the trinity of proportions, or the arithmetical, geometrical and the harmonical. In market terms this is a clue to the relationship which exists between the angle of lift in charted prices; the prices, and the extent, or time of market activity in days, weeks, months, etc.

Pythagoras taught further that there is a numerical relation in all phenomena: the harmonic intervals of numbers with sounds; the relationship that the square of the hypotenuse, in a right handed triangle, is equal to the sum of the squares on the other two sides; and more important, that angles of a sphere have specifically corresponding numbers, which are sensitive to those angles in space, infinity and time. The lift of charted prices does coincide with numbers at specific points in space, corresponding to price and time. In these observations is the entire basis of geometrical charts.

CHAPTER TWO

# FIRST STEPS IN CHARTING

Most of the various methods of charting market prices ignore the necessity for a constant balanced relationship between the elements of time and price. Usually one unit of graph paper represents one unit of time, such as a day or week, while two, five, or any convenient number of units is taken to represent one cent or one dollar. The observation seems to be that any unit relationship is satisfactory just as long as it is carried throughout the chart. This is not the case.

In geometrical charting the primary rule is; that *there must be an identical unit to represent both time and price.* Ancient geometry was principally concerned with geocentric and astronomic observation. It discovered that all natural phenomena is, in some way, concerned with circles, or cycles: such as the diurnal movement of the Earth on the axis, the 28 day cycle of the Moon around the Earth, and the cycles of the planets around the Sun. The circle, or cycle, was the basis of geometry; and, lines emanating from the axis of a circle, and the relationships of these lines on the circumference of a circle, are the first tools of geometry. They prove balance.

The 360° of a complete circle contain several cardinal, and many lesser, points. The major cardinal points are those which mark the four major squares of every circle, and those which mark the three major triangles of every circle. Fractional harmonics form the lesser.

A perfect cross of two lines, drawn through the center of a circle indicates the four cardinal points on the circumference; and, coincides with

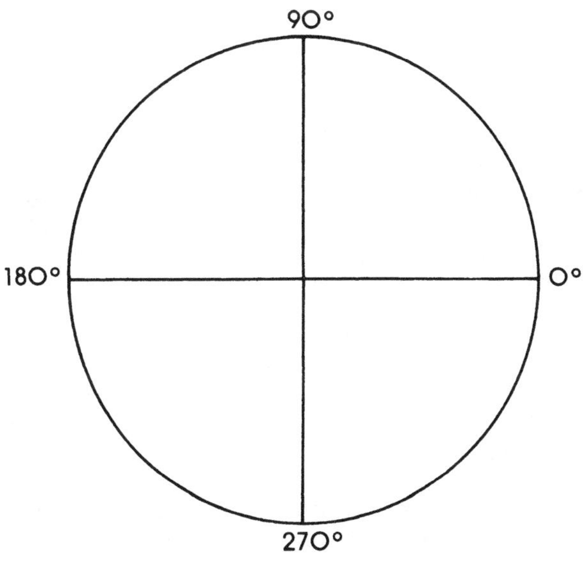

the four seasons of the year. A cross divides a circle into four equal parts, each part 90° or one half of 180° and a quarter of 360°. This 90° angle is the "square" unit, or the symbol of the meeting of force and resistance. Two 90° angles are the equal of 180°, or, the symbol of opposition and alternative. The point of 0° is always the beginning or place of origin, and the positive pole, while 180° is the negative pole; one is Self and the other Not-Self, the start and the finish, the top and the bottom. All degrees which divide 90 equally are related to "resistance."

There is another set of major critical points within a circle; from the major triangles. Where the first division was one of quarters or 90° angles, the second division is of 120° angles or thirds. These two divisions form the basis of all angles and division, of not only circles, but of

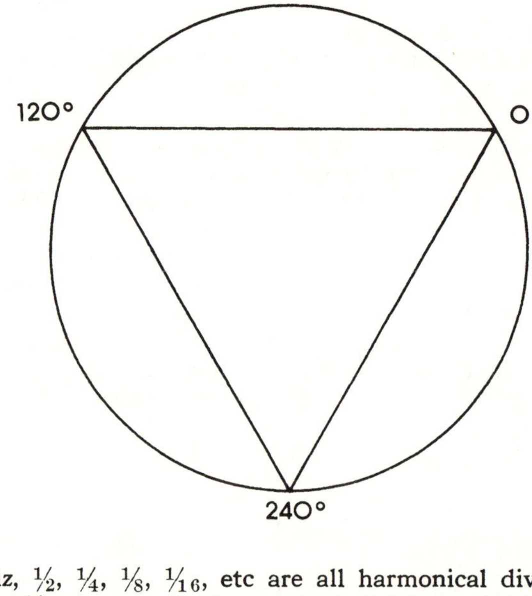


any unit, viz, ½, ¼, ⅛, 1/16, etc are all harmonical divisions of 90°, while ⅓, ⅙, 1/9. etc, are the harmonical divisions of 120°. The 120° angles, and their harmonical divisions, relate to co-ordination, harmony and balance. They are not only unifying but bring adjustment which relates to the ideal. So in zodiacal sign relationships the major triangles, or trines, tie earth to earth, air to air, fire to fire and water to water. In market charts, these units mark areas of market adjustment or areas and periods of consolidation in time and price.

The co-ordination of nature with these basic angles shows up in a variety of ways. Under microscopic examination molecules of copper, iron and quartz follow the major angles. Snowflakes, in myriads of major angle forms, illustrate the major angles. One twelfth of a year is one month; one twenty fourth of a day is one hour; one hour-sixty minutes: all are divisions of the trine, or 120° angle. Similar connection with the square or 90° angle can be noted. As Laotze said, everything exists for a purpose, and the virtue of everything is in its use; which can include geometry and market charts.

The sketch below illustrates the necessity for a market chart unit of time—days, months, etc—always being equal to the unit of price—one dollar or one cent. There is balance when A-B is equal to C-D. If A-B is one unit of price then C-D must be one unit of time. There is an immediate unbalance if A-B is one unit and C-D is three, or five, or ten units of measure. Most important rule of geometrical charting—that the arithmetical unit of measuring time and price shall always be identical.

Lack of space makes it impossible to offer illustrations why it is also necessary to show every unit of calendar time on all charts, instead of following the popular practice of simply indicating market days. Usually

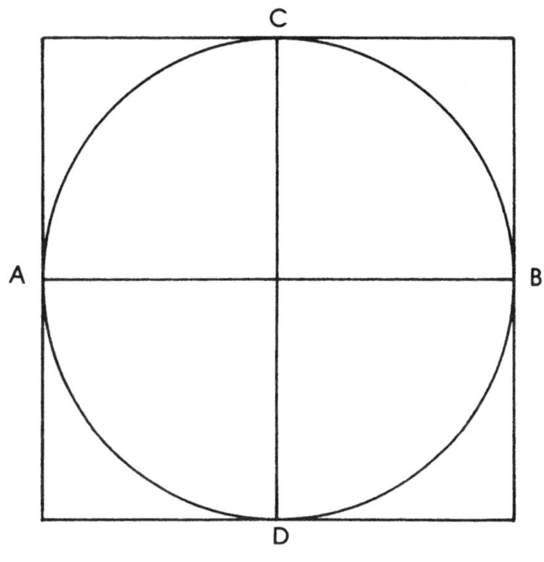


chartists provide no space for Sundays and those intervals when the markets are closed. Yet the student of economic cycles realizes that Sundays and holidays may halt the completion of such economic transactions as market turnover, but they do not halt a cycle of time. The forces which result in market statistics are operative 7 days a week and 24 hours a day. Forces behind the movement of money are not halted because most of the banks of the country are closed a large part of each 24 hours. So it is with market forces, they operate constantly. So charts must show calendar time, not market time.

In preparing charts it does not matter what unit of measure may be selected, just as long as it is followed throughout the chart. Use any type of paper from the 20 by 20 squares to the inch to the 1 by 1 square to the inch. The only point is to maintain a balance of units.

For general purposes the readily available graph paper of 8 by 8 squares to the inch is convenient to handle for grain futures, stocks and

Averages. In grain charts use one unit to indicate one cent, and one equal unit to indicate time—which will be a day, a week, month, or year, depending on the type of chart. On the 8 by 8 paper 1/8 inch will present one cent on the vertical scale, and 1/8 inch will mark a unit of time of the horizontal scale.

In security price charts 1/8 inch should represent one dollar on the vertical scale, and 1/8 inch represent one unit of time on the horizontal scale.

It is profitable to carry charts on the daily, weekly, monthly & yearly range of prices of every stock or grain option in which there is any interest. For most purposes, however, the charts can be limited to one daily and one weekly. Do not load up with a great number of charts. One hour of interpretation is better than ten hours of marking up high, low and close statistics. Enter the calendar days—or weeks—across the top from left to right, and the price range in the left hand margin from bottom to top. Begin all charts from the last major high or low. A space to provide for volume should be provided along the bottom of each chart.

CHAPTER THREE

# RESISTANCE, OBJECTIVE AND TREND

After a set of daily and weekly charts has been laid out, with a range started from either the last major high or major low, the next step is to enter the major angles. We want to estimate all the probable elements of the present and future price range, resistances, and price and time objectives. For illustrative purposes let us begin at the last major low. This low is, geometrically, the axis or center of a circle. However, price activity on a chart moves upward and to the right of the axis, so we can only use 90° or one quarter of the circle, illustrated in the sketch below. From point **A** a line is drawn to equal and parallel **F-B**, and then the

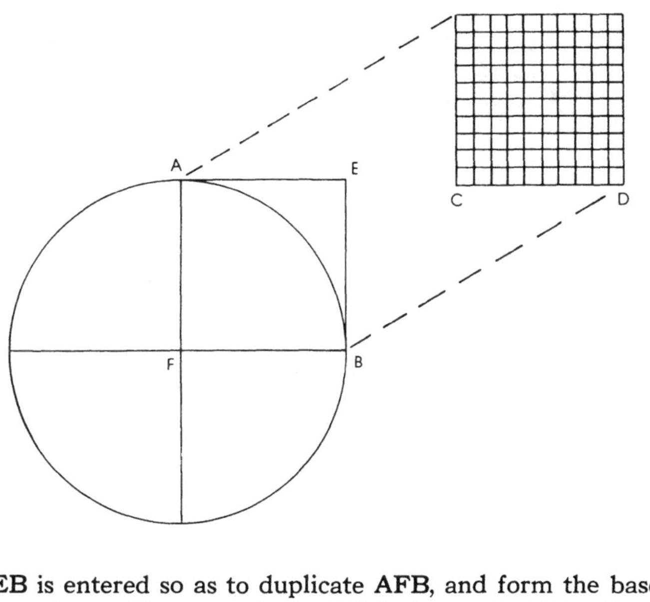


angle **AEB** is entered so as to duplicate **AFB**, and form the base figure for our chart form. The extension on **CD** is the result. Literally, **C** is the same as **F**—the axis of the circle and the point of the major chart low (when inverted, it is the major high).

According to the Pythagorean observation the degree units (angles) of a circle have numerical co-ordinates which are harmonical. In this instance the 90° from **A** to **B** represents 90 units of measure from **A** to **F**, **F** to **B**, **B** to **E**, etc. And it follows that the extended square on base line **C-D** must also be measured by 90 units on each of its sides. This square of 90 is our base unit in all market charts, except with minor exceptions in the daily.

On the opposite page are two sketches which illustrate the important angles of a circle and also the 90° segment. One indicates the manner in which the harmonics of 90° form four perfect squares in every circle. The other illustrates how four triangles form on the major harmonics of 120°. From the axis these points form angles of 90, 45, 22½, 11¼, 67½, etc in the squares, and 75, 60, 30, 15, 45, 90, etc in the trines. Note that 90 and 45 appear in both groups, indicating they are doubly strong.

Keep the entire gamut of these critical degree points of all the groups in mind, not only when computing time by days, or weeks, but in computing price and resistance. Think in numbers, rather than angles.

The points which are harmonical with the square of 90 signal resistance, and points of trend reversal, as their connecting lines extend to

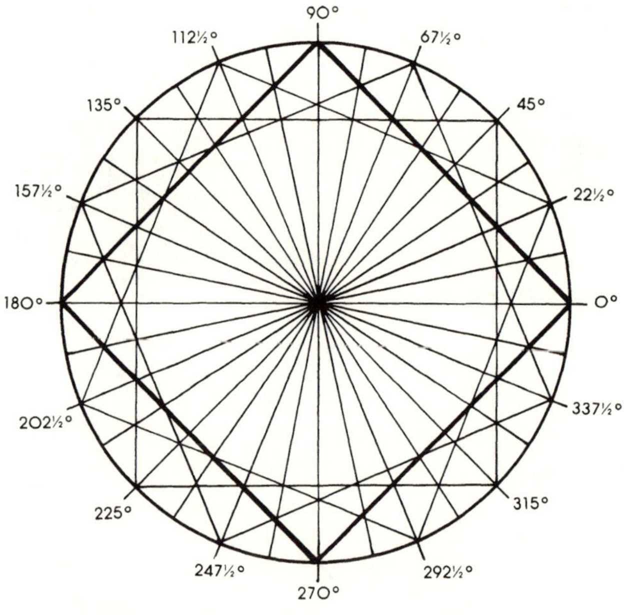


axial highs or lows. In time measure all harmonical points of 90, or from 0 to 360, represent days, weeks or months of resistance, from a major high or low. This coincides with the 88, 44 and 22 day cycles of Mercury, viz, 90, 45 and 22½, etc.

In other words, in measuring time count from a major hi or low in calendar days, weeks or months for critical areas in time.

The points harmonical with the trines also mark important areas in time and price, but the levels they indicate are related to that type of market action that accompanies periods of adjustment or consolidation.

The critical points of the two groups—square and trine—operate from 0, and also from any beginning, viz, a major low at 11 would locate the 45 point at 56 (11 plus 45) and not 45.

The trine points tie up in the approximate 365 day cycle of the Sun which marks 1 year.

The application of these critical points is now used in entering the lines from axial tops and bottoms in the square of 90. (See Plate 1 on the opposite page). The sensitive degree points are tabulated on the top and side margin of the graph. The lines from point **X**, the axial center, and also our theoretical low point, form angles which are not measured on the circumference 0–0, but on the sides 0–90, and 90–0. This is our foundation, a complete unit which is to be applied to every low, and inverted, to every high on our charts.

The strongest angle is 90°, coinciding with the vertical line of **X** to the top 0. The next strongest is the 45° angle, formed from the lower 0 to 90, or the line of 90. Points **E** and **E** are also 45, and are points of the

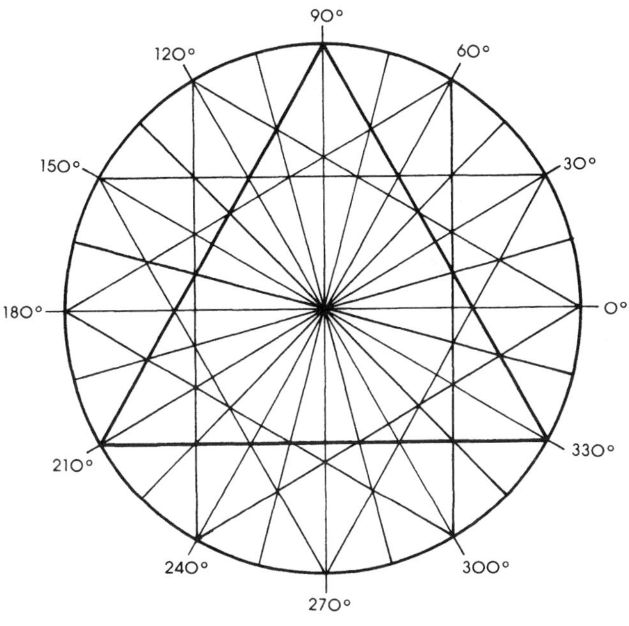


square within the square. As all the lines from the axis **X** are followed note how cross lines coincide with critical degree points. **X-D** is the 30 point line (measured across the top). On the circumference 0–0 is an angle of 71¼°. Note the minor resistance at 33⅓ points, and the major resistance at 67½, on the graph. In time (from left to right) these points are 11¼ days or weeks, and 22½. So it can be readily observed that the Pythagorean postulate proves out: that there is a harmonical relationship between angles and numbers, which, in terms of market charts, ties up the "lift" of the price structure with time and resistance.

In order to avoid the inconvenient and cumbersome necessity of entering the full square of 90 at every important top and bottom that materializes on our charts, a precision detail colluloid protractor is used and the critical points translated into angles by means of those tables which are entered at the bottom of Plate 1. Most drawing and draftsmen supply dealers stock them.

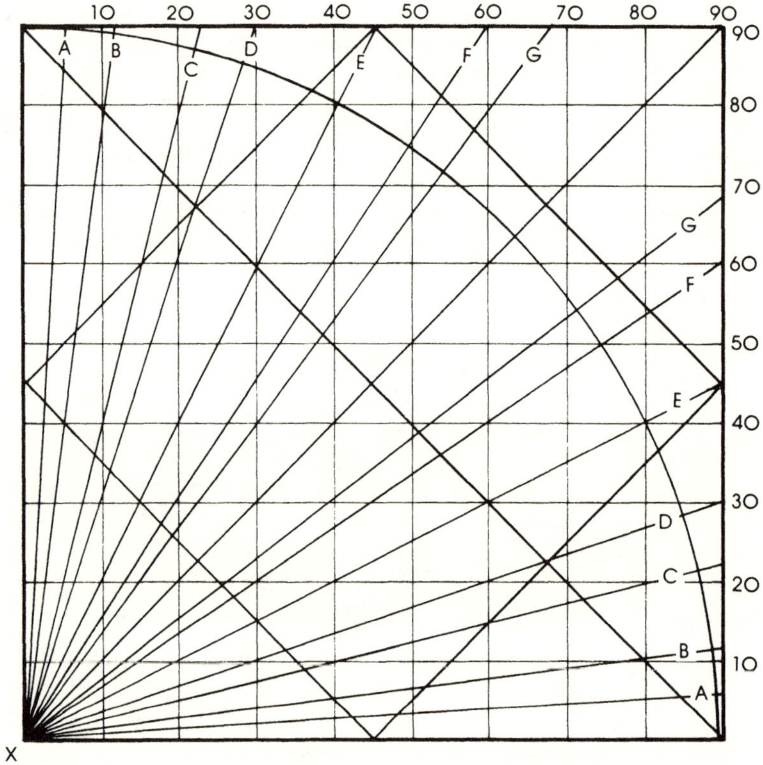


| *Top of Graph to Right* | | | |
|---|---|---|---|
| **X–A** | 5⅝ spaces | | 86¼° |
| **X–B** | 11¼ | " | 82½° |
| **X–C** | 22½ | " | 75° |
| **X–D** | 30 | " | 71¼° |
| **X–E** | 45 | " | 63¾° |
| **X–F** | 60 | " | 56¼° |
| **X–G** | 67½ | " | 54½° |

| *Right Margin Upward* | | | |
|---|---|---|---|
| **X–A** | 5⅝ spaces | | 3¾° |
| **X–B** | 11¼ | " | 7½° |
| **X–C** | 22½ | " | 15° |
| **X–D** | 30 | " | 18¾° |
| **X–E** | 45 | " | 26¼° |
| **X–F** | 60 | " | 33¾° |
| **X–G** | 67½ | " | 37½° |

Another method, which is even simpler after a little practice, is to use the scale of measurement below. Count from the axis **X** upward, or to the right, as the case may be.

| *Vertical Scale (Right Margin)* | | | | | |
|---|---|---|---|---|---|
| 5⅝ | spaces | —16 | over | 1 | up |
| 11¼ | " | —16 | " | 2 | " |
| 15 | " | —12 | " | 2 | " |
| 22½ | " | —16 | " | 4 | " |
| 30 | " | —12 | " | 4 | " |
| 45 | " | — 8 | " | 4 | " |
| 60 | " | —12 | " | 8 | " |
| 67½ | " | —16 | " | 12 | " |

| *Horizontal Scale (Top Margin)* | | | | | |
|---|---|---|---|---|---|
| 5⅝ | spaces | — 1 | over | 16 | up |
| 11¼ | " | — 2 | " | 16 | " |
| 15 | " | — 2 | " | 12 | " |
| 22½ | " | — 4 | " | 16 | " |
| 30 | " | — 4 | " | 12 | " |
| 45 | " | — 4 | " | 8 | " |
| 60 | " | — 8 | " | 12 | " |
| 67½ | " | —12 | " | 16 | " |

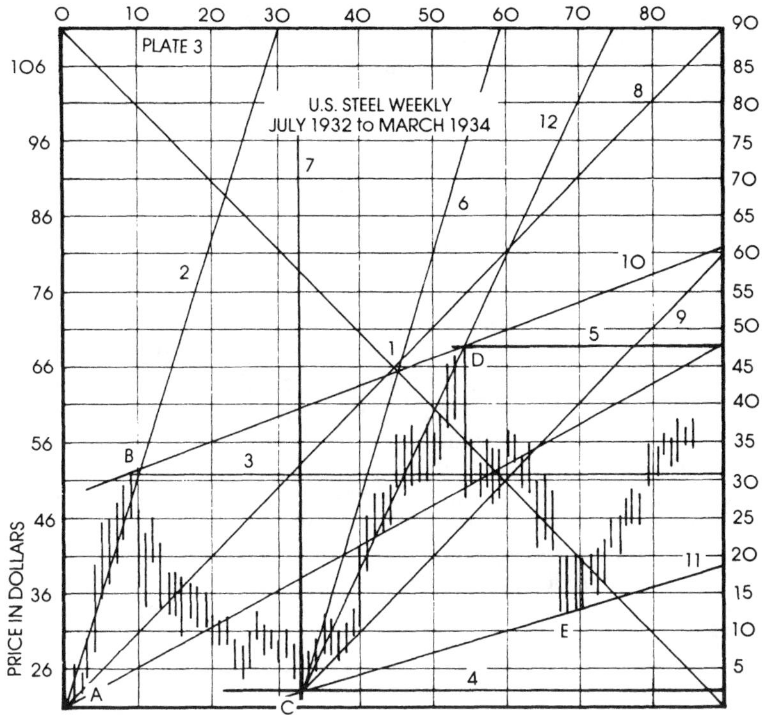


| | |
|---|---|
| A – July '32 low | 4 – Horizontal from low C |
| B – Sept '32 high | 5 – Horizontal from high D |
| C – Feb '33 low | 6 – 71¼° 30 spaces (7) |
| D – July '33 high | 7 – 90° on C |
| E – Oct '33 low | 8 – 45° on A |
| 1 – Axis '32 low | 9 – 45° on C |
| 2 – 71¼° 30 spaces | 10 – 18¾° 30 spaces (B) |
| 3 – Horizontal from top B | 11 – 18¾° 30 spaces (C) |

12 – 63¾° – 45 spaces (C)

We can now enter the important lines on the weekly charts. For illustration note the weekly range chart of U. S. Steel Common on the opposite page (Plate 3). The first procedure was to align the axis, of the square of 90, to the low point of July 1932 at A. As soon as this is done the price is tabulated in the left hand margin, and the major lines of 90, or 45° angles, are entered at 0, through the exact center at 1, and from A to 90. Then the top and side points of 30 and 45 are entered. For simplification all but the top 30 is deleted on this Plate 3. These lines illustrated that the major resistances in price were, on the upside, where the major lines cross at 1, or $64 in price and 45 weeks in time, and, on line 2 at 51¼ (the top scale of 30 points added to the low of 21¼ at A).

As the weekly range of prices rose along this line no other lines were necessary until the September 1932 top at B.

As soon as the top was made the horizontal top line at 3 is entered. Then the line 10 through B and 1 was drawn. Then a line parallel to 2 is entered through 1, and the 45° angle down from B. Just as long as a weekly or monthly range stays above the line of 90 it is bullish; and, conversely, as long as the range travels under the line of downward 90 it is bearish. The line of 90 from B was not penetrated until the point of convergence of vertical 7 and parallel 6 was reached at C. At C then, a new base line 4 was drawn; line 11 is entered parallel to line 10; and, the line of 90 at 9 entered. This signalled that the weekly range holding above line 11 was bullish & if it held above the 90 line 9 the objective was; first, the high 10 line, and, a price within "orb" of point 1 or $64. The high materialized at the high line point D, just under $68, in July 1933. Note:—line 12, drawn from C through D, strikes at 76 on the top margin and scale, 44 points added to the February 1933 low at point C are 67½ and the July 1933 high on U. S. Steel.

Study Plate 3 carefully; and, with the material already discussed, set up charts for ranges over the past. Facility in locating the manner in which resistance points and objectives can be computed, in advance, will soon develop. The more points of crossing at one week, or at one price, the more important is that point. Always be generous with lines. Have more than you need, rather than too few. Always carry all the major lines from every important top and bottom. Begin with the line of 90, or 45°, and when a line is entered above this major line always enter a line below, at the same degree point.

A great number of different combinations of angles and lines can be applied to every chart. If the fundamentals already discussed have been thoroughly grasped each combination can be worked out to a logical conclusion.

Study the manner in which duplications recur on all charts, and how when one square of 90 is completed the succeeding square will develop duplications, not in exact prices but in geometrical form and reflected by the price ranges. Note that parallelograms and forms of squares and rectangles prove out, as complete moves of prices occur. A major objective can be anticipated by drawing lines from double and triple tops and bottoms. When making such extensions run the 90 point line upward from the first bottom, then the 45 top point line on the second bottom, and if there is a third bottom, enter the 22½ point (top) from it. Where these lines converge will mark a major point of resistance in time and price. Conversely, from tops, the lines go down.

Keep in mind that the sensitive angles coincide with critical points of prices. For instance, if a stock makes a major low of ten dollars per share you can immediately outline its major and minor resistance points in days, weeks and months, and in price. Simply take the major degrees such as 15, 30, 45, 90, 105, 135, etc, and add to the major low; viz, 10 plus 15 equals 25, 45 and 10 equals 55, etc. Count the days and weeks in the same manner.

In entering lines and angles on the charts always strive for geometrical balance. When the 90 point line is drawn from a low, balance it with a 90 point line from a top and note where they cross. If a 90 point line, or any other, is drawn from a bottom, parallel it by the same point line UPWARD from the preceding top. The three sides of a parallelogram—the two parallels for two sides and a line extending from the top to the bottom—give clues to when and where a move in prices will be completed. In the same manner, watch for duplications in time and price in the ends of the parallelogram. This "boxing" of the price range is very effective to locate when a move is completed, and to aid in finding objectives and price levels. They are most effective on the weekly charts, but should be looked for in the daily charts also.

Above all, recognize the necessity for flexibility in entering lines. Always be ready to apply variations of the basic rules.

CHAPTER FOUR

# THE DAILY CHART

Where the weekly, monthly and yearly charts of market prices—all set up according to the illustration used for the weekly chart of U. S. Steel, in the preceding chapter—are the foundations for interpretation of the major trends, probable tops and bottoms, plus points where turns are probable, the daily chart gives a closer and more enlarged view of the minor trend. In practice one is a supplement to the other; the weekly and monthly charts indicating the long trend perspective, and the daily charts the minor trends.

Plate 2 shows the daily range of the Dow Jones Industrials and the Dow Jones Rails from January 1st, 1933 to September 29th, 1933. A supplementary aid—a one point, Point and Figure chart of the Industrials—is also included.

Note that the rule of one day for one dollar is followed. Also, every calendar day occupies one unit—Sundays, holidays and, periods of closed markets, are all shown. The square of 90 and the line of 90 are not used, except in the minor trends. In the daily charts we confine ourselves to actual trend lines on the highs and lows.

The tops A and B are the horizontal base lines. Until those lines were broken at C the market was not in a bullish trend; as, even though strong implications had developed on the weekly and monthly charts, the confirmation on the daily chart was not complete. Then when A and B were penetrated, base lines were entered across preceding lows shown at 1 and 2. Note how these bottom or low lines held through the repeated attacks in prices at 3, 4, 5, and 6 on both Averages, indicating that the trend was fundamentally bullish up until the apex of the major triangulation, D-E-3, was broken out of at E.

On the intermediate trend of the Industrials, from C, through D, count the days in terms of our observations of critical points, viz, 5¾, 7½, 11¼, 15, etc. As soon as the 90 point and day passed, resistance became increasingly heavy. On the major point of 105, or day, an important high was made. Then go back and count the days from the time the resistance across A and B was broken at C, and apply the same critical points. The top in prices occurred on the 90th day following the breakout at C. Apply this principle throughout all types of charts.

Always keep the geometrical fundamental of balance, plus the harmonical relationship between degrees, points, days, months, and weeks, in the forefront of attention. At the same time be prepared to allow an "orb" of "aspect." That is, allow for discrepancies in all computations up to about 2½%. An objective of 90 days or 90 dollars can carry a range of points 2½% higher or 2½% lower. 2½% of 90 is 2¼, so the range would be from 87¾ days, weeks, points or dollars, to 92¼ days, weeks, points or dollars. Apply this general percentage "orb" to all computed objectives and resistance points.

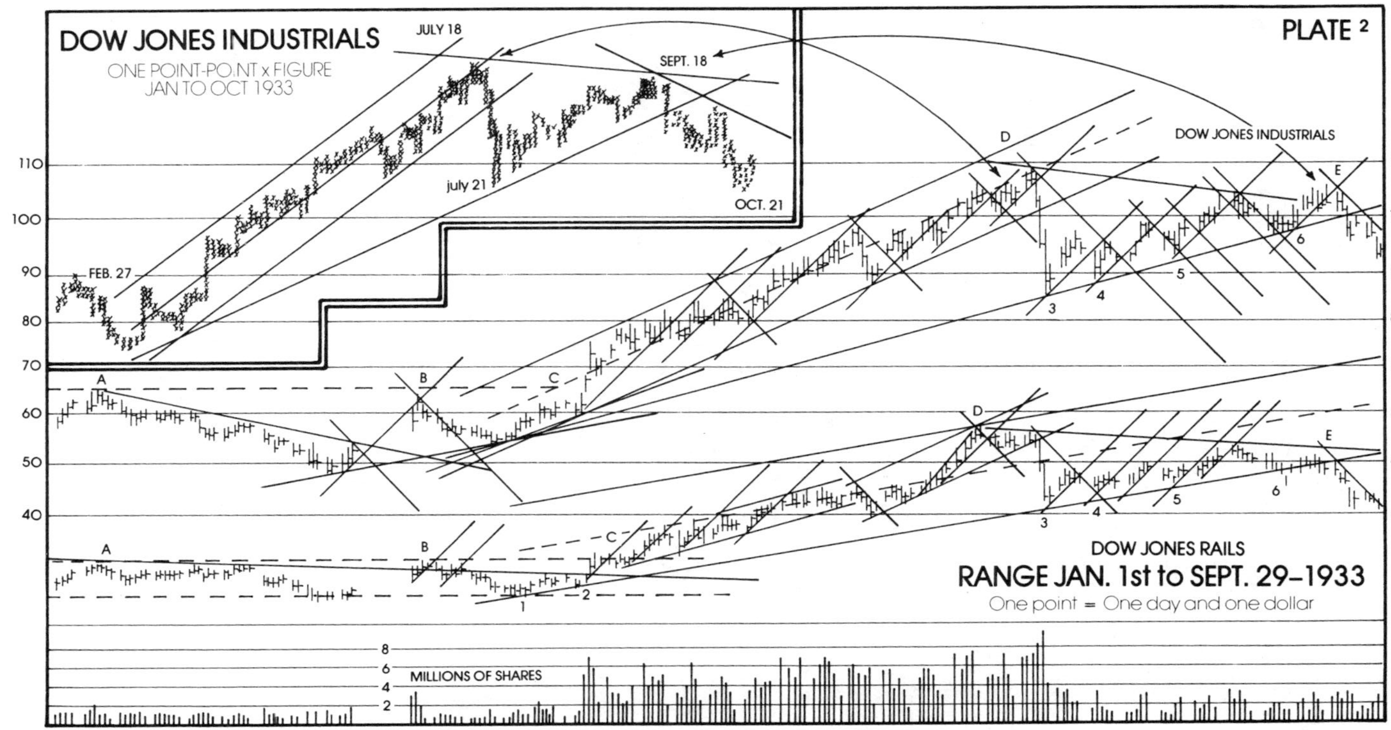
PLATE 2
DOW JONES INDUSTRIALS
ONE POINT-POINT x FIGURE
JAN TO OCT 1933
JULY 18
SEPT. 18
FEB. 27
july 21
OCT. 21
DOW JONES INDUSTRIALS
DOW JONES RAILS
RANGE JAN. 1st to SEPT. 29–1933
One point = One day and one dollar
MILLIONS OF SHARES

In the penetration of trend lines or previous highs and previous lows on the daily charts, the percentage rule can generally be ignored for the "one point" rule. This rule applies to all chart points not computed on the degree points of the major angles, such as trend line points, highs and lows, the applications of the Dow Theory, and in interpretation by the Point and Figure method. The rule is, allow a one full point penetration before accepting the implication as definite.

The volume of transactions is important. It should be charted on all stock charts and on the charts of the Averages, and if possible, on grain charts. In Plate 2 the volume of transactions is entered on the bottom of the chart, with daily vertical lines indicating the number of transactions in millions of shares. Follow through this chart of the volume to see how the volume increased as the trend line on the lower side of the channel was broken near D. As point 3 was approached, volume decreased; the pressure of liquidation was passing, with prices preparing for a recovery. But as volume did not materially increase on the upside movement along the succeeding higher bottoms at 4, 5, and 6, the bullish trend was not convincing.

Note that all minor tops and bottoms carry an upward or downward line of 90, or 45° angle line. As long as the minor trend holds above this line the minor trend continues unchanged. When this angle is broken a reversal or consolidation occurred. Use of this angle on every daily chart is of tremendous value in short term trading operations. But remember, like the major trend lines across tops and bottoms, it only is effective on charts which follow the arithmetical balance of one unit for time and one unit for price; and, that every calendar day is provided for and shown on the chart.

As with the weekly charts, experiment and test charts of past action with these methods.

CHAPTER FIVE

# SUPPLEMENTARY HELPS

If every investor and trader will keep an up to date and carefully drawn set of charts, for every grain option and stock in which he is interested, he will be amply repaid in greater profits, plus a new basis of confidence. Such charts, used in conjunction with a subscription to a technical and advisory service, will enable him to not only maintain a market perspective, but help him to crystallize his observations into profitable action. The better a trader understands his reasons for making commitments, the greater are his chances to attain profitable results.

As a minimum, use a weekly and a daily chart for every grain option, and stock, in which you are interested. Then, if possible, supplement the individual charts with charts of the Rails and the Industrials in stocks; and in grains, carry a corn option if you are trading in wheat, or wheat if you are interested in corn. The Dow Theory where the primary and intermediate trends are involved, is very useful in not only stocks, but in grains. In stocks, use the daily Industrial Averages, and the daily Rail Averages as compiled by Dow, Jones and Company. In grain, use the option of wheat to replace the Industrials, and the option of corn to replace the Rails. Always use options which run out in the same month—like September wheat and September corn. The Chicago Board of Trade options work quite effectively in this form.

The Dow Theory is a method of market interpretation developed by the late Charles H. Dow of the Wall Street Journal. It was later amplified by William P. Hamilton. In recent years there has been a pronounced tendency to read certain implications into the theory which it was never designed to convey. Basically, the Dow Theory is a very useful method of interpreting the intermediate and primary trends only. Its use in minor trends is of little value. For everything that may be implied under the Dow Theory study the book by Robert Rhea, entitled "The Dow Theory."

One of the oldest professional forms of charting market prices is the Point and Figure Method. It is an excellent supplement to the geometrical charts, when the chartist wants a separate check on the important levels of accumulation and distribution, resistance points and the main trend. The method pays no attention to calendar or market time; it is not concerned with the volume of transactions. Its entire purpose is to follow the price movement. The upper left hand portion of the chart comprising Plate 2 illustrates a one point chart which was compiled by the Point and Figure Method. It will be noted that units of price less than one, such as the fractions of ⅛ and ¼, are ignored. In compiling these charts the general rule is that full point changes are entered on the chart by x marks. Starting on a day a stock moves between 11½ and 12⅞, the figure to be entered is an x at 12—the only full figure in that range. Then, if the stock advanced through 13, into 14, an x is entered in the space above the x at 12. If, however, the stock price churns between 12½ and 13¾, and then breaks through the full figure 13, move to the next vertical column of squares to the right and enter x at 13. The data for these changes may be taken from quotations in newspaper financial pages, or from the daily range charts; but the only satisfactory source, so as to follow all fluctuations, is to take the data directly from the tape.

Refinements of this method are used in a great many ways. There are one point charts, half point, quarter point, three point and the five point. All forms have their own particular use and contribute to market interpretation as a whole. Considerable data on this method is available.

Various mathematical forms have been developed to produce automatic "buy" and "sell" signals. The most noteworthy of these are labeled "running average" devices. These may consist of two lines running on an arithmetical chart. As long as the same trend continues these lines hold a parallel position to each other. At a major turning point the one line will cross the other. A popular method of computing such a pair of lines is to use the daily close for one line and the average of the closes of the preceding week for the other line. Sometimes the average of the preceding highs, or lows, are run on one of the lines, or a third, and sometimes even a fourth line is added, each line carrying various combinations of figures.

But, to supplement the geometrical method of charting there is one basic method which overshadows all others in usefulness. It lies in a close study of the tape itself. On the tape is recorded every transaction in the market, with every fluctuation in price, every item of volume; or, in brief, a completely detailed moving picture of each stock and the market as a whole. Watching every movement of price and volume on the tape, without retaining the perspective of trends revealed in the charts, is *a danger few observers can guard against.*

# Section IV

CHAPTER ONE

# FIRST STEPS PUTTING IT TOGETHER

The purpose is to try to define or at least make an estimate of the probable future trend of speculative markets, notably stocks and commodities. Is the major or long term trend upward or down? It was upward in stock market averages from 1932 to 1965, approximately 33 years, but something else in terms of individual stocks then and since. And this basic upward trend actually was a series of intermediate upward and intermediate trends constantly making marks on affairs. For example, from 1932 to 1937 was an intermediate upward trend; from 1937 to 1942 was an intermediate downward trend. And within all intermediate trends, whether upward or down, are constant minor trends. One of the initial steps in developing estimates of trend prospects is to define precisely what these trends may be.

It is amazing the ignorance which prevails on these elementary factors. Most brokerage salesmen, and there are exceptions, seem bred to markets pointing upward in their incessant search for orders to buy something. Declines are admitted but always as temporary setbacks. In turn, most of their customers think always somewhere the trend will be upward. An old wheeze is that security prices always eventually go higher and compare the Dow-Jones Averages of 1897 with those of recent years. One quick answer is that Pennsylvania Railroad in the days of World War I was the final word as a deluxe, income paying blue chip of blue chips. To soften what may seem to be a put-down note that Haloid, the poor and struggling cousin of Rochester photo industry moguls for many years now has grown to some stature as Xerox. The trend must be defined by the position of the Averages and the issues being scrutinzed as possible candidates for purchase or sale.

An intermediate trend usually has five phases, three in its direction and two corrective minor trends. Thus, the intermediate upward trend usually has a relatively small initial upward phase such as July to September 1932 on the Industrials, a minor downtrend of varying length such as September 1932 to February 1933. The second upswing minor trend follows as from March to July 1933. The second setback carried to near the end of 1934 from which the third upswing and blow-off phase made a peak in early 1937. It is almost axiomatic that the third phase of an intermediate uptrend is the largest and longest because by that time people feel the future profit prospects are both unlimited and assured. As one technician often said when people demand stocks in a third upward phase he always was happy to please them and sell out all the stocks he owned.

The years 1973 and 1974 marked the most devastating market losses than any two year interval since the early 1930's. Vicious declines occurred in 1966 and 1969 in terms of the popular Averages but comparable rebounds followed rather quickly to restore preceding values and the Over-The-Counter market did not collapse. In our annual trend projection estimates issued and copyright in December annually for the forthcoming year cyclic estimates again proved themselves. For example, 1974, at the end of 1973, was a chaotic prospect after February was out of the way, as Jupiter would begin to move toward a square of Saturn. And in April the weak trine of retrograde Uranus to Saturn would begin to shift to a square. These are bearish elements intensified by the Node moving through Sagittarius all year, the opposition area to our Gemini critical point. Forecast projection: firming early in the year, late May peak, September low.

One of our market turning points, in the relation of Jupiter and Saturn at 126°, converged in early February in a weak manner, because Saturn was retrograde at the time; again in late September when Saturn was direct but Jupiter was retrograde; and again in December. At the latter, Jupiter was direct but Saturn again was retrograde. However, very significant factors were included in the December data: Uranus had moved into Scorpio and was working toward a trine with Saturn, Jupiter was nearing a trine to Saturn which also would be a trine to Uranus; and, the opposition of the Node to 8° Gemini culminated late in the month. With the stock market at the lowest point since the panic of 1962, and within shouting distance of the highs of 1956, it was the framework of a classic low.

The 1974 market trends confirmed the 1932–1965 upward major trend had reversed to a major downward trend in its first decline made in 1966. However, an intermediate upward trend correction should follow, and be of considerable magnitude in prices and quite lengthy in time.

In the projected trend estimates for 1975, issued and copyright in December 1974, a peak was anticipated May 29th when a strong square of Jupiter and Saturn occurred, and repeated in late June and again in mid-July. By December, and Jupiter turning direct the 11th, the upswing was projected to resume.

Recall in the foregoing that the September through December 1974 cyclic data was turning into bullish. Meantime the technical structure of the stock market had developed that the primary or major trend, in terms of the Averages, was down. The widely acclaimed 1973 high on the Industrials, which never had been confirmed by the Transport Average, had been a false move which had collapsed into the panic condition of 1973 and 1974. What caused the panic? Of course there are a multitude of reasons and explanations are comfortable,

*But We Are Going to Ignore Everything But Astro-Cycle Timing*

and then look for confirmatory action in the trend and market amplitude.

So charts of market statistics are the next step in putting it together. If the section on setting up the geometrical chart form needed has been quickly read and not carefully studied step by step retracement may be irksome at the moment. Here is a simplified explanation. That it may seem repetitious may clarify some factors which may have been hazy. The application is for the more prevalent daily chart of price ranges, to aid in grasping the method.

The elements which mark the transaction of any exchange, in individual stocks and in any commodity, are the end result of an auction resulting from many sources. The elements which motivate these sources are operating twenty-four hours a day and seven days a week, although the auction market may operate for only a few hours a day in a five day week. In order to visualize some of the actual phenomena of market trends and the waves of activity *a daily chart must show every calendar day. Where Saturday, Sundays and holidays occur blank spaces show in the chart.*

The second fundamental is to recognize the immutable law that a visual record of price trends accepts the premise that time and space, or amplitude and distance, must be equal. Thus, *if one space representing one calendar day in the horizontal plane is one-eighth inch, then one-eighth inch is mandatory in the vertical plane* to represent one unit of price. The unit prices most commonly accepted are one dollar for one point in a stock, one cent as one point in grain, etc.

The two initial fundamental premises are: on daily price range charts all calendar days must be shown, and the width of the space comprising a calendar day is exactly the same as the height of the space representing the unit price.

CHAPTER TWO

# TIMING ELEMENTS

As a market tool, charts afford an interpretive insight which is cultivated by experience. In themselves charts do not forecast but market action revealed by charts presents means of interpretation to the observer from which tentative projections may be formulated.

Means of estimating the duration in time and the objective in price of a market trend, whether upward or downward, is the goal of market analysis. The multitude of factors involved have so few absolutes on which to base judgment the process is more an interpretive art than a science. However, if market charting is adapted to those mathematical laws of trigonometric relations which apply to all problems of time and space many factors of science may be applied, and interpretation fortified.

Trigonometry involves angles. An angle is generated by two lines, one stationary and the other rotating. In market charts the stationary line becomes a major high, or conversely a major low. Angles are measured in radians or in degrees. A circle divides into 360 degrees; when it is divided by two lines at right angles through the center the angle at the center is 90 degrees. The circle then has four quadrants of 90 degrees each. Note that the angle defines the number of degrees. If a radius of a circle is bent on the circumference of the same circle the subsequent arc marks an angle termed a radian. A radian is 57° 17′ 45″ or 57.2958°; pi is 3.14159, so pi radians is 180°; pi/2 radians is 90°; pi/3 radians 60° The harmonic divisions of 90° are ½ or 45°, ¼ or 22½° and ⅛ 11¼°. The harmonic divisions of 60° are ½ or 30°; ¼ or 15° and ⅛ 7½°. In our market charting we view these degrees as angles of the amplitude of trends of prices and the distance velocity in time and price. Thus there is the velocity of either an advance or decline in prices defined in degrees, and in addition there is a harmonic relation in the angle of velocity to the waves of prices. A rise which adheres to a trend channel of approximately 15° degrees reveals price resistances at 15, 7½, 3¾. To illustrate: a stock in a 15° uptrend has an upside breakout at 35, major resistance will be at 35 plus 15 and lesser resistance at 35 plus 3¾ and 35 plus 7½, as long as the 15° uptrend channel remains intact. Another stock is priced at 20 where a series of minor highs have occurred and it leaps out of this established resistance at an apparent 45° uptrend angle. Probable resistance to the new advance will appear at 20 plus 45, 22½, 11¼ and 5⅝. This works out as 20 plus 5⅝ or 25⅝, 20 plus 11¼ or 31¼, etc.

The velocity of prices changes forms one insight to the power of the momentum which eventuates probable exhaustion. A directed magnitude of this velocity then can be estimated by vectors. A major vector has within it a series of smaller vectors which often differ in magnitude and direction. And a charted market trend of daily prices has a major or general trend within which are a number of minor trends of varying magnitude and duration. In charting the applications to use are polar coordinates where a vector is defined by a magnitude and an angle, or vectorial angle. In this usage the 90° harmonics apply to the angle of the price trend with its time factor of days to reach exhaustion, and 60° harmonics apply to price resistance.

Tentative market price objectives which form subsequent resistance areas often are revealed in advance by imposing triangles of varying vectorial values. An example is to project one angle on the low close day in prices and a lesser angle on the first preceding low close day; the crossing will estimate exhaustion in time and price. To illustrate—the Dow Jones Industrials have an average velocity of 45° or one-half of pi/2 radians. The associated price resistance factor then is 60°.

Below are tracings of a daily chart of the Dow Jones Industrials from March through June 1960. In Chart A the day of the highest close is at (B); the highest preceding close day is at (A). As soon as the setback from (B) brought a close below the previous low close day (**X**) a tentative projection was entered. A 45° angle was entered at (A) and a 60° angle projected from (B). The convergence at (C) indicated a potential base between 600 and 605 the first week in May.

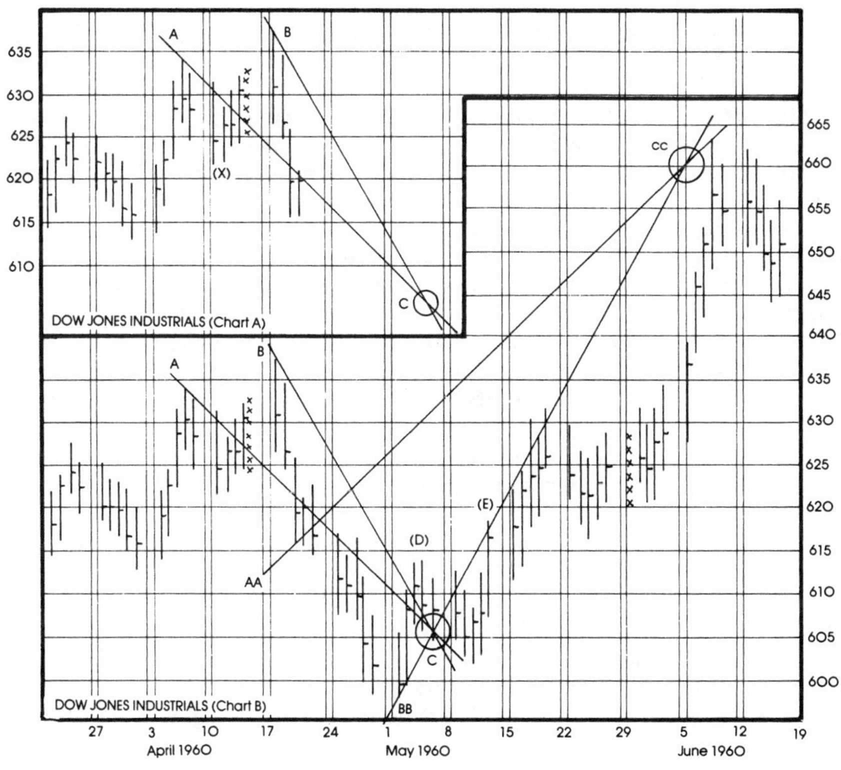

Price Chart B duplicates Chart A until after mid-April. When the early May projection was confirmed, when the close (E) was above the preceding high close (D) the low close day at (BB) was imposed with an upward 60° angle and at the preceding low close day (AA) a 45° angle was entered. This presented a tentative possibility of the Industrials achieving the 660 level in early June. Note also the arithmetical resistance approximations; for example, from (BB) the first surge was 598 plus 15, the second surge 598 plus 30; the eventual top approximately 598 plus 60.

In practice the precision of the foregoing is often upset by unusual surges of mass psychology. As a defense several measures are constantly used to fortify judgment and guard against changes in the apparent normal of market action.

Refer briefly to the circle in quarters with its quarter square on page and then the subsequent page depicting the full 90° square with the more critical angles. The daily application has been outlined leading up to the significant applications.

Often there is a search for repeating cycles by statistics and then there is the constant reference to the economic cycle. The former is the often heard 9 year cycle, the 11 year cycle, the 18 year cycle or the 54 year cycle. Recently the unprecedent extreme low of 1976 in Sun-Spot activity, and its wide range of effects related to weather, harvests and humans, has relegated its average 11 years cycle to prospects of a major cycle of 80 to 90 years. It has been a wide search for statistical cycles with indifferent success.

The latter or what is labeled the economic cycle avoids being trapped by a time factor. Conveniently it is often a theory. A prospective demand such as housing is pump-primed with capital and credit. Contracts are let and in a certain period of interval business supplying materials expand as producers convert raw materials. So it goes, one factor sprouting another, until the "cycle" runs its course; it might be a brief year or two, or it might run for many years. Its greatest problem is a trail of bad judgment. Statistical cycles constantly skate the surface trying to average a factor from past statistical ebb and flow. Astro-cycles have been carefully rejected as faulty to start with, or in more recent years since the puritan mystique has lost its thought-control powers, most research has been confined to five or ten years of research effort, and then rushing into print. The factors become overwhelming by their large number instead of being sifted down to potent and workable simplicity. Certainly it has faults of omission.

Someone claims astro-cycles all converge to the same position once briefly only every 26,000 years. It may be true but the point is no two cycles are exactly alike. Jupiter has its 12 year cycle but in the 12 years its apparent retrograde and forward paths aspect other astro-cycles without simple statistical repetition. And markets reflect timing factors which are not precisely symmetrical as mathematical cycles, a statement which seems elementary but is noted here because a degree of elasticity has to be accepted. A market may be projected to top out at noon Monday and doesn't; it tops out late Tuesday, etc.

The Earth takes 365 days to go around the Sun, and the Moon makes

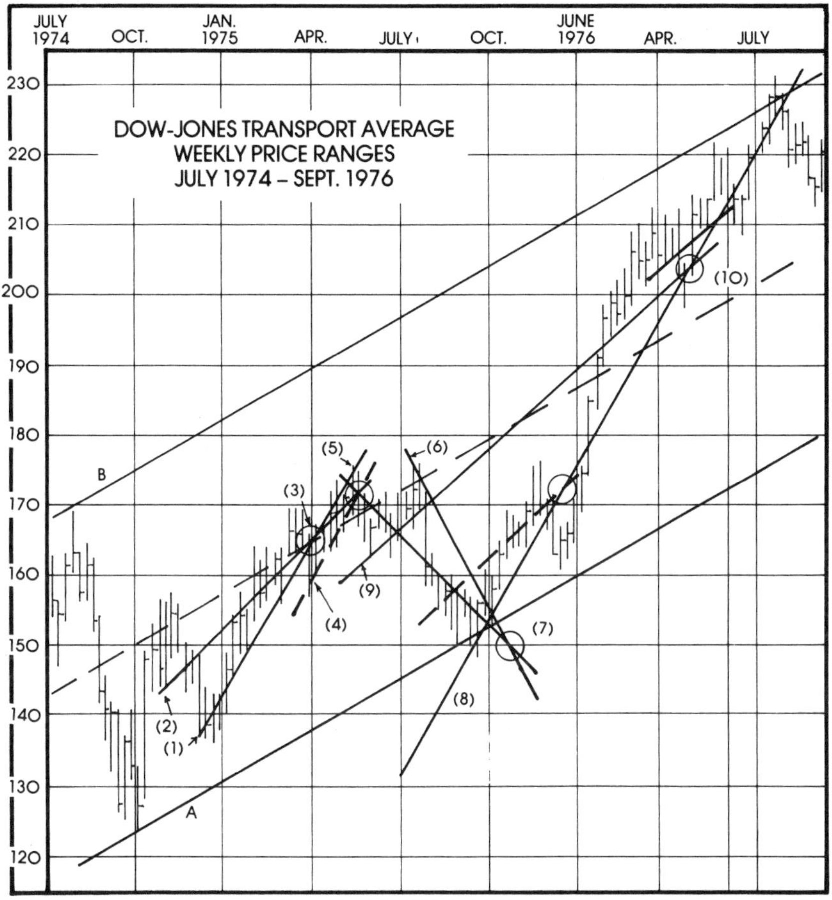


13 revolutions around the Earth in 364 days, or 7 revolutions in 91 days. A satisfactory graphic presentation is to use the 360° circle, divide it in four 90° parts, and keep repeating the 90° square at highs and lows. Related is the phenomenon of markets staging price surges of 11 calendar days (9 market days) which relates to the 88 day cycle of Mercury interlaced with the 365° and 28° and 91° factors.

The most comprehensive and valuable charts are those of the weekly ranges. Useful are monthly range charts. The tendency is to get trapped with so many daily range charts interpretation gets lost. Application of the weekly range chart exhibits many useful elements. In the foregoing, 1974 cyclic data noted a rebound and substantial upswing in the stock market was in the prospect. A possible September low was the alert with late December the probable kick-off into the upside. This portended a base in October to December inclusive. The Dow-Jones Transport Average chart is used for clarity and space limitations.

CHAPTER THREE

# CHARTING THE PRICE RANGE DATA

This chart is the weekly ranges of the Dow-Jones Transport Average from July 1974 to August 1975 inclusive. As discussed, the September low was anticipated late in 1973. When the October rally and subsequent minor setback stabilized at higher levels than the September low, confirmation of the September low was implied. The two parallel 30° lines (line A & line B) were entered, from the October low close week and the July high close. Added was the dashed line exactly between the two which was to represent market vitality, viz, ranges below the dashed line would be weak, on the line normal strong, above the line excessive strength inviting distribution.

Next step was to enter the initial 45°–60° bisecting projections (in very volatile moves resort has to be made to try a 60°–75° combination). Point (1), for the 60° line, was at the bottom of the LOW CLOSE week of the setback in early December. Point (2) 45° from the November low close week. The convergence (3) was in the center of the tentative range of closes at 166 the first week of April. When the April tentative objective was approached the market was very strong (above the midline slightly) but nevertheless reacted as due, up about 30 points on the move from point (1). (Recall that 30 points or degrees are a critical zone).

The reaction was quickly absorbed and the low close week range had a tentative (dashed) line (4) entered which converged in May at a 172 close. This was the zone of the cycle high of the year prospect we already discussed. Also the 172 prospect was precisely 45 points above the October extreme low close week of 1974. It was time to move out. On the move the actual high close of the year was made on the weekly ranges the second week of July after seven weeks of lower prices and swinging congestion.

Confirmatory weakness in late July invited placement of downward angle lines (5) and (6) which converged at (7) approximately on closes 22 points down or half of the critical 45 points resistance, implying a strong market and higher levels. However, the major underside upward 30° line from the October low close week was under test for six weeks but without a close making a penetration of it. Conclusion: take out any short positions but defer buying pending more well defined market prospects.

At this juncture an upward 60° line was placed at the bottom of the low close week (8) (at 150–151) and a 45° line at the bottom of the low close week PRECEDING the high of late July, which converged at 204–205 in April 1976. As it was close to the major 60° resistance, and the price ranges substantially above the median line, headlong buying demand was coming in. Prices could attack the upper side of the channel, marked by (B), but the third upward phase was in full bloom and the upward intermediate trend was blowing off. It was time to be a nice fellow and feed out the stocks they were bidding up in the fever to buy.

This same step by step procedure, if followed exactly as detailed, can be applied to any stock or commodity which is active and has participation.

Spend no time experimenting with different scales of measure and papers. The 5 spaces to a centimeter, with each centimeter accented, is available at almost all stationery stores. Cheaper grades, but the same precise measure, are in every super-market and variety stores in 8½″x 11″ that carry school supplies. Sheets can be glued together as needed. The uniformity afforded gives facility with projections and the relatively small size is easy in picking out prospective moves. Plastic protractors (180°) of the 6″ variety are a must. The 15, 40, 45, 60, 75 and 90 degree lines can be scratched and inked on them.

To lay out paper and set it up to begin a chart sometimes is a roadblock. The data is not available or takes too much time to search out. Sometimes the plea is that it means going through weeks of back issues. BARRON'S is the most available source of weekly price ranges and a subscription to build a file of copies is a good investment. Most speculators with a background of working at market action keep charts of the daily price ranges of several commodities and stocks. These charts can be readily used to run the WEEKLY ranges which comprise the secret of this method.

Without a variety of personal daily charts and pending an accumulation of price range data from BARRON'S or other sources, the following are useful.

DAILY BASIS STOCK CHARTS, issued weekly
TRENDLINE 1 month—4 issues $27.50
345 Hudson Street
New York, N. Y. 10014

3-TREND SECURITY CHARTS Single copy $7.00
(weekly ranges; do not confuse with Cycli-Graphs)
Securities Research Company
208 Newbury Street
Boston, Mass. 02116

The Trendline charts are daily ranges which must be translated to our weekly ranges and the week's close included. The Security Charts are weekly and cover about two preceding years. Unfortunately it is in a semi-log scale which is useless for our purpose. But weekly ranges may readily be placed on our chart form. Volume also is valuable and might be used also. On both of the above a good magnifying glass, in order to get closes exactly, is needed.

Our comments and illustrations have been confined to upward trends.

Often more profitable in a shorter length of time are short positions, or short against purchases which cannot be liquidated for one or several reasons. All techniques are of course reversed. For example, the basic working unit of the 90 square unit with its angles from an apex at the lower left hand corner is turned so the apex is at the UPPER left hand corner. This is obvious but years ago readers sometimes reported difficulty in applying this device.

A very few readers in the 1930's, when this work first appeared, critically rejected it. In several cases these critics were asked to send charts that the problem, if any, might be overcome. In every case they had intruded their own ideas or habits of charting, usually by distorting the scale so that the price unit was not exactly equal to the time unit. Sometimes the weekly closes were carelessly entered or left out entirely.

As a final comment this text requires step by step study. Casual readers will be unable to follow parts of the text, and proceed to take a critical stance this is just another book. It is not, but some key factors are scattered through the text. Herein is the complete skeleton of the results of 54 years of research and study which included 45 years as a professional analyst. Many long time clients have insisted for the past ten years that my personal methods of interpretation should be recorded for others who are sincere students searching income and security in perhaps the most exploited money melange in our society—speculative markets.

CHAPTER FOUR

# ESTIMATING PROSPECTS FOR A LOCALITY

(Business Trends, Weather, Earthquakes, Disasters)

Locate from an atlas or other source the latitude and longitude of the location to be examined within a degree of each. Refer to the World Map page to define the proper sign zone. For example, let us take Pittsburgh, Penna. The approximate data shown in a Table of Houses (Simplified Scientific T of H by Rosicrucian Fellowship, Oceanside, Calif. covers 0° to 66° latitude.) is 40° N. Latitude, 80° W. Longitude. From 60° to 90° W. Longitude is the sign Capricorn. On the companion USA map 80° W. is in the Aries Dwadasamsas ruled by Mars Pluto (action, steel, iron, etc). The count of West Longitude is counter-clockwise beginning at Greenwich 0°. But the count within Signs is clockwise. Thus 90° W. Longitude is 0° Capricorn with 80° W. Longitude 10° Capricorn.

To be meticulous, which is superficial in this instance, we can intrude the Pyramid correction of 1° 7½′. This means that 90° W. Longitude becomes a trifle less than 89° and Capricorn 10° then is slightly less than 9°. Turning to the Table of Houses under 40° Latitude and 9° Capricorn on the 10th house cusp we find 9° (page 214) and apply the data to a chart form.

In Raphael's Ephemeris for 1977 we use January 23rd data as the beginning of the biggest winter storm in many years. The data is for noon London but adjustments are not needed; it is entered in the proper houses. See chart.

Ruler of the 10th is Saturn in the 5th and retrograde in Leo. The tables of planetary signs and houses makes this position an 8th house, with 10th house mixed tones, active in the 5th house. On January 23rd Saturn was sextile Pluto, square Uranus, trine Neptune, quincunx Mars, but exactly biquintile the MC with Mercury rapidly nearing a conjunction with the MC. This is a more devastating major storm potential than in the famous and costly affair of 1888, and similarly, the smaller storm of 1918; Saturn was in Leo also in both of the latter.

Putting together some of the key words to the foregoing we have: In winter the long angle of the Sun's rays on the Earth keeps the temperature of the Earth's atmosphere at low ebb. Leo is a Fire sign ruled by the Sun and Saturn in Leo makes the Earth colder than normal; in the 5th house depresses the welfare of the area of the sign it rules (Capricorn), generates hardship for women and children, reduces speculative activity and public confidence and can be very depressing to business and government. The key words of each aspect and planet can exhibit the various problems and imply the final outcome, as

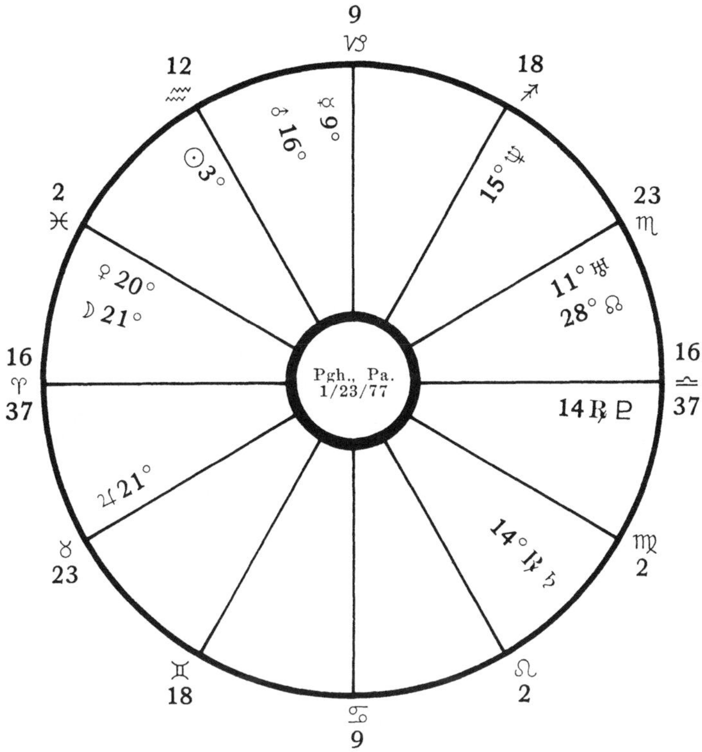


changing aspects are followed in the ephemeris for subsequent weeks or months.

In a locality chart the house each planet is in may be significant. And when a planet is in aspect to one or more other planets its potency is enhanced. So-called good and bad aspects are of little significance. The square and the trines are significant but are of differing values according to the natures of the planets involved. An opposition of Venus and Jupiter lacks the activation of such an aspect as Mars to Saturn, for example. And the generally ignored biquintile group are the action triggering group, second only to the conjunctions to the 1st, 4th, 7th and 10th house cusps, viz Asc., Nadir, Desc., and MC.

In our example chart the forepart of 1977 presents a disturbing business, health and weather prospect for the Capricorn rulership area. The often mitigating influence of Jupiter is quite meagre in Taurus and lacking any close aspect of planet array. In early January Mercury was retrograde in Capricorn activating the aspect array centering on Saturn in Leo. Then Mars entered Capricorn, Mercury turned direct to cross the MC, with its 144° (biquintile) aspect to Saturn January 23rd and its converging sextile to Uranus on the 26th. Mercury Uranus aspects at sensitive chart points always indicate wind and when closely aspected are the key to tornado paths; Saturn indicated cold.

The Mercury Mars in Capricorn combination continued active. February 2nd Mars at 24° and Mercury at 18° triggered the Saturn in Leo aspected array on the MC Leo locality zone in the section from about 140° East Longitude or about 20°. At about 40° North Latitude the Tables of Houses gives us 20° Leo on the MC and 11° Scorpio on the Asc. Reported from Northern Japan were heavy losses and damage with about 10½ feet of snow over a period of 48 hours. Uranus was conjunct with Asc. ruling the 4th with property damage large and sudden. Thus abnormal planetary arrays in Capricorn and centered in Western Pennsylvania late in January 1977 had varying effects in other areas. For example, Saturn in 14° retrograde in Leo approximates the MC of the Japanese storm area. Another, with the same data:—Place Uranus 11° or 41° East Long. 10° No. Lat. Scorpio on the NADIR (4th cusp) of the 11° MC; 2° Aquarius Asc. ruled by Uranus, with Mars the trigger. Ethiopian leadership assassinated in a major revolt.

Sometimes indications are observed which seem to indicate an important change in local weather and nothing occurs. The forces might be compared to a loaded gun which has all the elements to produce shooting a bullet. Nothing happens without trigger action. Note carefully trigger aspects conjunct or close aspects from the quintile group to the angle house cusps, exact degree of the preceding lunation, and occasionally the parallel shift from North to South and South to North of Mercury, Venus and Mars.

To aid initial facility in interpretation, experiment with these key words.

| *Sign* | *Nature* | *1st Decan* | *2nd Decan* | *3rd Decan* |
|---|---|---|---|---|
| (♈) ARIES | stormy | showers | calm | hot |
| (♉) TAURUS | quiet | quakes | wet | stormy |
| (♊) GEMINI | nice | rain | temperate | threatening |
| (♋) CANCER | warm | humid | normal | windy |
| (♌) LEO | torrid | humid | quiet | wet hot |
| (♍) VIRGO | moist | hot | humid | rain |
| (♎) LIBRA | changeable | nice | temperate | moist |
| (♏) SCORPIO | storms | cold | static | turbulent |
| (♐) SAGITTARIUS | windy | humid | placid | stormy |
| (♑) CAPRICORN | wet | dry | temperate | moist cold |
| (♒) AQUARIUS | moist | damp | changes | stormy |
| (♓) PISCES | wet windy | nice | wet | turbulent |

The key-words helpful in identifying effects of a planet on weather and seismic trends, perhaps over-simplified as strong aspects amplify or neutralize the simplified effects, are:

( ☿ ) Mercury—wind; ( ♀ ) Venus—temperate & mild; ( ♂ ) Mars—turbulence, heat; ( ♃ ) Jupiter—mild, warm, sultry; ( ♄ ) Saturn—cold, precipitation; ( ♅ ) Uranus—sudden changes; ( ♆ ) Neptune—strong winds often easterly; ( ♇ ) Pluto—focuses, amplifies.

The aspects between planet positions and orbs of effectiveness are significant.

A general rule is an orb of 5% each side of center, viz, 90° 4½°, etc. The opposition (180°) is 9° each side of center, and the conjunction is the same. All orbs in the Quintile series are limited to 2°.

The activity of aspects may appear confusing as the three classes actively used overlap or are in the same degree (°). Interpretation experience quickly develops the application in a specific situation.

Harmonizing aspects (traditionally favorable) are: semi-sextile 30°, sextile 60°, trine 120° and 180°–30° or 150° quincunx.

Activating aspects (traditionally unfavorable) are: semi-square 45°, square 90° and opposition 180°; conjunctions (0°) are of planet's natures. The 22½° and the 180–45, which is 135°, often are useful.

The triggering aspects (also marking reversals in some market trends) are the Quintiles related to one fifth of the 360° circle, or 72°. For example, the root is 9, twice 9 is 18, twice 36 is 72, 72 plus 18 is 90, 72 plus 90 is 162, 162 plus 18 is 180 (except for the latter this series is useful in estimating peaks of intensity between major planets in close aspect). The second series of quintiles begins with: 18 plus 9 is 27, twice 27 is 54, 54 plus 72 is 126, 126 and 54 are 180. (market trend low points often appear at these angles between planets). And particularly in weather and seismic data 72 x 2 is the 144° angle.

Since the attempts to develop push-button thinking by computer have appeared, which may employ hoards of people collecting statistics to feed the monsters, they may locate recurring cycles of weather conditions, business trends, etc. Some of the outcome have cost a mint of money with the only practical result many people are employed at nice wages. Most of the tentative cycle rhythms usually relate to the following planetary conjunctions of geocentric computations.

Saturn Uranus every 44 plus years, Jupiter Uranus every 13 plus years, Jupiter Saturn about 20 years, Jupiter Pluto 12½ years, Uranus Pluto 127, Saturn Pluto 33½, Saturn Neptune 36, Jupiter Neptune 12 plus, Uranus Neptune 171, Pluto Neptune 492 years.

In the late 1930's I had temporary access to detailed daily weather data for a mid-west area for much of the period from 1910 to 1920. Before the time involved made it necessary to abandon the project to return to making a living a definite Jupiter (rain) and Saturn (cold) combination was fruitful. The base was the Rotational Jupiter-Saturn Conjunction chart of 1921 (included in this work on another page). This figure was super-imposed on a MC locality figure and around the circle daily ephemeris transits were compared approximately 20 years from the 1910–1920 specific daily weather figures. It was not possible to bring the research to compare other data time spans.

Weather and seismic conditions have a marked effect on business, health, and all the factors which involve society. In examining clues to conditions and probable future trends we can outline months and years in advance by day to day computations from an ephemeris which covers the periods being examined. It is a mathematical exercise according to the framework of methods and procedures offered here. It is about as occult, crystal balling, or ESP concentration as driving an automobile on a freeway.

Procedure to examine the business prospect of a specific area follows much the same methods we have applied to weather estimates. Major difference is that house positions become more significant and the angles (1st, 4th, 7th, 10th) recede from dominance (see section on house rulerships).

As an example we shall briefly review the late 1920's and early 1930's. During those years I was traveling extensively in the USA and Canada and was daily aware what went on in widely separated localities. Modern history is conveniently rewritten often to erase "non-essentials" and loses a lot of truth in the process. Where did the Crash and Depression get its start? It was a combination of many things. After Europe in the 1920's, and the sad conditions of Germany, Russia, etc., there was a huge effort by private capital to stabilize the situation. It tried but lacked the resources to generate capital, credit and money. The effort was made but it collapsed.

Refer to an ephemeris (preferably Raphael's) for each year from 1928 to 1933. Set a series of locality charts of the house positions only for a half dozen centers across the USA, such as New York, Detroit, Chicago, etc. For quick review note positions of Jupiter, Saturn and Uranus only on these charts beginning in 1928. Saturn is in the MC area of Sagittarius MC charts of the West and is moving East. Late in 1929 it is established in Capricorn moving to a square of Uranus in Aries in a first house ruling the 12th.

In 1930 Saturn clings to Capricorn in square to Uranus and Jupiter moves into Cancer squaring Uranus and opposing Saturn. Through 1931 the situation hangs on until early in 1932 with Saturn moving East to Aquarius out of Capricorn. In 1952 there was a somewhat related situation of square and opposition. But it occurred in entirely different sectors than the 1930's in sign positions and locality houses. Saturn at MC is the clue to the depression of the 1930's.

Incidentally, if a person super-imposes a chart of birth on a selected locality the effects of that environment often will be indicated. To illustrate locality factors refer to data on the mid-1930's for the upper mid-west. Saturn by forward and apparent retrograde was on the Ascendant opposing Neptune, Uranus afflicted also but in the second house, etc.; it was depression compounded by drought situations. Many ultimately profited immensely but the majority suffered, particularly those with their personal chart positions related to the Saturn in Pisces locality chart. Some years ago a person who consistently experienced living and career problems in New York City, with an afflicted 4th house at the NYC MC in Capricorn, moved to Idaho where the Sagittarius MC was conjunct his Jupiter. In the subsequent several years he realized excellent business, health and social success. Of most value though is the means to adjust to the problems of a locality through an insight into area syndromes, in relation to the aspirations of the person exploring the situation.

## EARTHQUAKES

### A Long Range Forecasting Procedure

The Earth is a pulsating mass with changing weather, constantly shifting ocean tides, plus thousands of earthquakes every year. Most of the latter never are sensed but occasionally the exception occurs and generates devestation and loss of human life. Recent estimates are that earthquake fatalities in 1976, from the Guatemala, China and Turkey epicenters, were the largest since the year 1566 A.D. To include the March 4th, 1977 major losses in Rumania intensifies the problem.

Science explains the mechanics of earthquakes is a movement of the earth's crust which is from 2 to 30 miles deep. Under the crust is a hot liquid mantle about 1,800 miles deep and then into the center a hot metal inner and outer core about 2,200 miles thick. Forces below the crust may fracture and break the crust to form mountains, volcanic eruptions and earthquakes. In some instances the surface crust has been damaged and a break or fracture exists which marks weakness and repeated tremors occur; then quakes become a regular situation.

The point under the earth's crust where the greatest pressure develops is the epicenter where the earthquake begins. However, greatest damage sometimes occurs many miles away by what are called seismic waves. A homely example is watching a pie baking in a hot oven with the top crust without any vent holes. After a time the pressure in the pie begins to mount, the crust bulges and subsequently the edges burst open or the thinest area of the crust pops in a small explosion. On the earth's crust the increasing pressure causes the bending, dropping and sometimes breaking of the surface, to generate the quake.

Very little has been accomplished in the efforts to forecast the time and place of earthquakes. In some areas earth tremors occur almost daily and are under constant study. The San Andreas fault in California extends about 650 miles along the Pacific Coast from north of San Francisco south. In the sparsely populated mountain area of southwest Oregon–northwest California in 1926–27 severe earth tremors aroused panic to find the cause. During the years to follow a forecasting formula was attempted. Like everything else it has limitations, but the way estimates weeks, months, and in several instances years in advance, have been confirmed in approximate time and place, is of interest. Although asked for my method of interpretation I have avoided explanations: these notes present the simple procedure, with the hope others will test the method.

Usually most observers are interested in a specific area where the latitude and longitude are readily apparent. The forecaster wants to scrutinize where and when a quake may occur. The location is unknown. Here is a means of overcoming the problem.

Soon after mid-1976 Raphael's Ephemeris for 1977 was issued the initial result was to scan the cyclic prospects day by day. The first crisis area appeared on February 24th in which Uranus, Saturn and Mars were in the same degree but NOT the same signs. Uranus in Scorpio was square Saturn in Leo and retrograde; with Mars in Aquarius opposition Saturn and square Uranus. This is earthquake weather if a trigger is produced.

Where a quake generates major losses in human life and property the first house of a locality chart usually is heavily involved. All the angles are significant in locality interpretation but where loss of life and extensive property damage occur the ascendant (cusp of the first house) are involved. Therefore in our initial example to locate the geographical place where quake action might occur both the MC (cusp of 10th house) for longitude and the Ascendant for latitude have to be searched out.

Involved primarily are Uranus in 11° Scorpio, Saturn retrograde in 11° Leo and Mars 11° Aquarius. If our interest is confined to one area, such as the United States, reference to the World Zone map 139 W. Longitude (11° Scorpio) is in Eastern Alaska, and the only MC location in North America, as the other signs are Leo and Aquarius. With 11° Leo the position is 131 East Longitude suggesting Japan, the Philippines, etc, while Aquarius 11° is 49 West Longtitude through Greenland and Eastern Brazil.

Before searching Ascendants at 11° degrees for each it should be noted most of the serious earthquakes rim the entire Pacific Ocean shores and islands. From New Zealand north around the Bering Sea and south down North, Central and South Americas is more or less quake prone. The only other major zone in recent years is Eastern Europe in the area of 40° to 45° North Latitude and 20° to 50° East Longitude. The latter "rings a bell" that the Aries-Taurus MC locality in that area of North Latitude has a Leo Ascendant.

Now it is a simple matter of locating in a Table of Houses in the Latitude of 45° as a beginning for 11° of Leo on the Asc. This is located and shows 28° Aries on the MC. In the column for 46° North Lat. the 11° Asc. has 26° Aries on the MC. On the Locality map 26° to 28° Aries is 26° to 28° East Longitude. This would show formation of a possible epicenter where internal pressure begins to build at approximately (we have avoided minutes by dealing only in degrees of latitude and longitude) 46° North Latitude and 27° East Longitude. This center is 50 to 100 Miles north of Bucharest, Rumania.

If this is the where, the question is when? There must be a trigger where any of the pressure build-up could explode. Mars at the 7th cusp ruling the 10th and part of the 4th promises heavy property damage and government losses. Saturn at the 1st (people) rules the 6th afflicted is prospect of many death and health hazards. Uranus in the 4th gives promise of an entirely unexpected event requiring help from other countries. Therefore a trigger point is serious. The first one is the Sun crossing 11° Pisces on March 2nd, and then the Moon conjunct Saturn and the Asc. March 3rd. On the 4th Mercury is at 3° Pisces after completing the 162° quintile to Asc. Saturn for the big test; if anything is to happen it is due March 4th, 1977.

On March 8th, 1977 Mercury was 120° from Uranus and 150° from Saturn. Using 130° East Longitude and North Latitude (10° Leo on the Locality map and Saturn on the MC) a quake occurred below of Japan Sea. This action is attributed to a reflex of the same February 24th aspects.

Rumania Quake

46 N 264 East
March 4, 1977

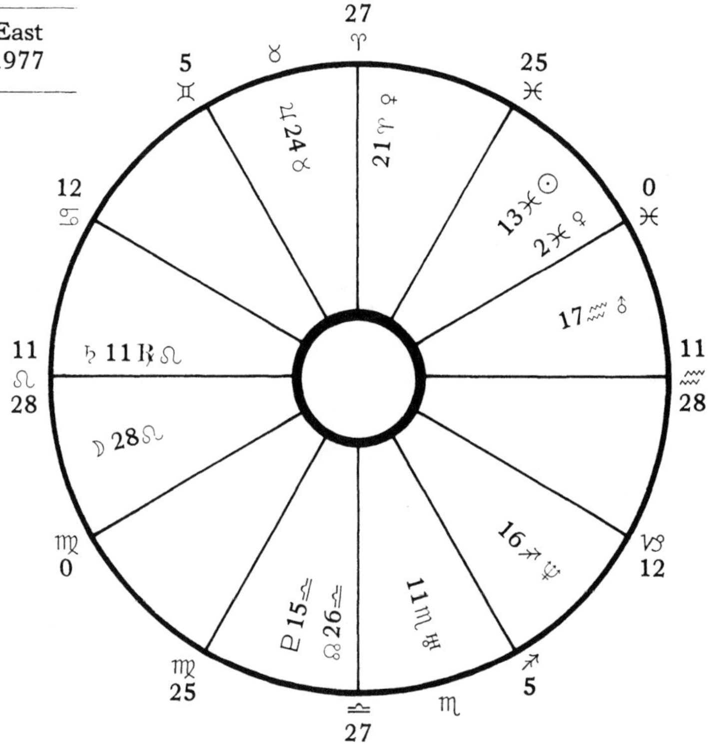

Epicenter reported 95 miles north of Bucharest.

## MAJOR MODERN EARTHQUAKES AND THE RICHTER SCALE

The most commonly used method for describing earthquake intensity is the Richter Scale.

The system, devised by C. F. Richter and later refined by Richter and Beno Gutenberg, measures the magnitude of a quake on a logarithmic scale using readings from a pendulum seismograph.

Each number represents an intensity about 10 times greater than the preceding number—an earthquake rated 7.5 would be 15 times greater than a shock measured at 6 on the scale.

A Richter reading of 1 to 3 would be a light tremor; 3 to 4, minor damage near center; 5–6, moderate damage near center with injuries unlikely; 6 to 7, felt over large area, heavy damage near center with injuries possible, 7 to 8, widespread damage, fatalities probable; above 8, many buildings destroyed and large number of deaths and injuries.

Richter readings have been used to evaluate all major quakes in the 20th century.

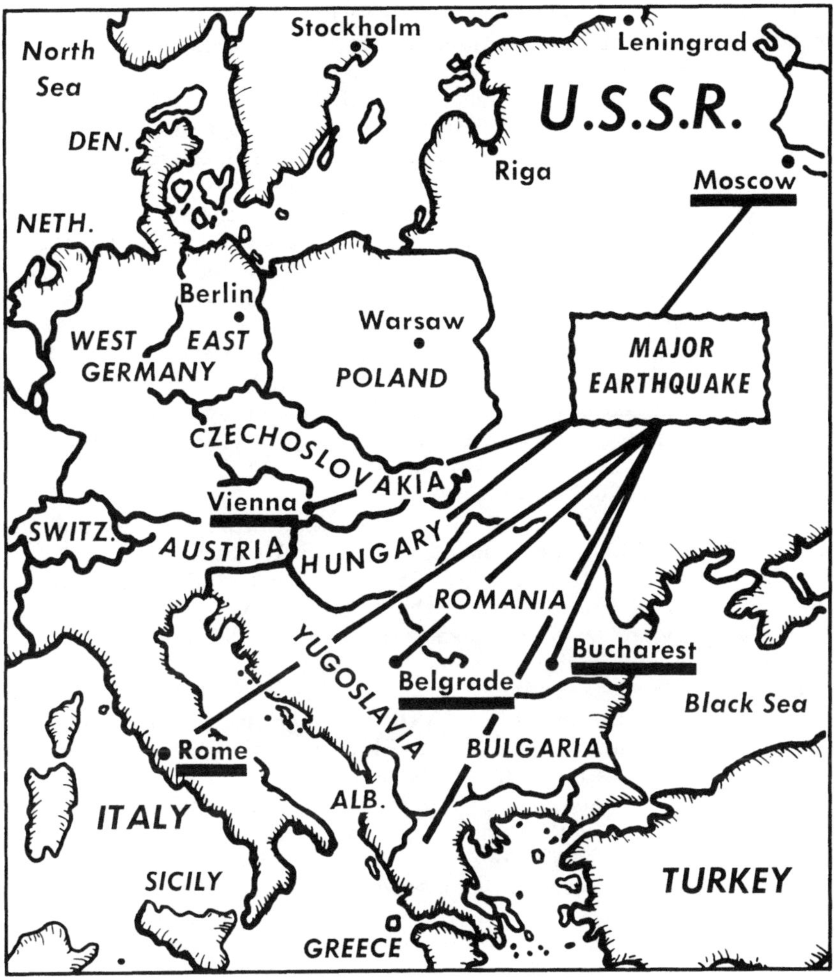


| *Place* | *Date* | *Richter* | *Deaths* |
|---|---|---|---|
| New Madrid, Mo. | 1811–1812 | 10* | ?? |
| San Francisco, Calif. | April 18, 1906 | 8.3 | 452 |
| Valparaiso, Chile | Aug. 16, 1906 | 8.6 | 20,000 |
| Kansu, China | Dec. 16, 1920 | 8.6 | 100,000 |
| Tokyo, Japan | Sept. 1, 1923 | 8.3 | 99,330 |
| Non-Skan, China | May 22, 1927 | 8.3 | 200,000 |
| Japan | March 2, 1933 | 8.9 | 2,990 |
| Chillan, Chile | Jan. 24, 1939 | 8.3 | 28,000 |
| Southern Chile | May 21, 1960 | 8.3 | 5,000 |
| Alaska | March 27, 1964 | 8.5 | 114 |
| Guatemala | Feb. 4, 1976 | 7.5 | 22,778 |
| Near Peking, China | July 28, 1976 | 8.2 | 300,000 |

* Estimate by Frank M. Wolley in the "People's Almanac."

The problem of earthquakes has persisted for centuries and the efforts to define the time and place of occurrence goes on. My work in the subject has been incidental as a phase of economic causes. For centuries astro-cyclic data applied to quakes has been issued. Much of it has involved quarterly Ingress charts applied to areas which might be suspect. Then charts based on timing comets, eclipses of both the Sun and the Moon, and conjunctions of resulting charts with Fixed Stars have been used. To examine the material can become quite a laborious exercise. However, as scores of quakes and the reported data on them are applied to the same procedures as outlined here for locality weather prospects the charts always exhibited fair results. Here is a recent example.

On November 23rd, 1976 a major quake began in Eastern Turkey in the mountain area near the Soviet and Iranian borders with the final death toll estimated in the thousands. The location approximated 40 E. Long. 39 N. Lat. for most loss, but the center probably was northeast of there in the most mountainous area. Anyway, for illustration purposes the above will suffice.

The Longitude of 40 East is 10° Taurus and at 39° N. Lat. and the Asc, is 17 plus of Leo, the nadir or 4th cusp is 10° Scorpio. Saturn was 16° Leo at the Asc., Jupiter at 25 Taurus in the 10th, Uranus conjunct the cusp of the 4th in 8 Taurus, the Node nearby in 1° Scorpio and Mars, Mercury and Neptune in the 4th. Tension had been brewing for several weeks with such a combination assailing the 4th, 1st and 10th cusps. The trigger was the lunation (new moon) of November 21st conjunct the 4th cusp and Mars. Also the Moon had just passed a conjunction with Uranus. If explored the lunation solar eclipse of October 23rd may have some build-up effects, as it occurred at 0° Scorpio.

Oddly enough a quake occurred November 24th 100 miles east of Bermuda, or about 77 W. Long. 26 N. Lat. (MC 17 Capricorn, Asc 25 Aries). Then on the 26th of November a Pacific Coastal area from Eureka north to Crescent City suffered a quake, which was 5.8 on the Richter scale, and compares with 8.25 in the San Francisco quake of 1906. The Eureka Crescent affair was 124 W. Long. 41 to 42 N. Lat., which has an MC of 26° Scorpio and Asc. from 3° to 2° Aquarius.

Quakes have occurred historically in virtually all locality MC signs, but as noted before, concentrations of planets centering in the Taurus Scorpio signs are quake prevalent (one or the other at the MC). However, these pressures having intense aspects to the angles of other areas signal major disasters. Examine three events in Far East areas. First, the quake July 28th, 1976 centered at Tangshan, China, 40 N. Lat. 118 E. Long., MC 28° Cancer ASC. 23° Libra. Second, on August 18, 1976 at Mindanao, Philippines, 7 N. Lat. 134 E. Long., with MC 4° Leo conjunct Saturn and Asc 6° Scorpio conjunct Uranus and the Node. A quake, plus a tidal wave, then over 20,000 homeless. And third, on September 12th, 1976 at Okayomas, Japan, 35 N. Lat. 134 E. Long., a typhoon with 4½ feet of rain in 5 hours, at MC 13° Leo conjunct Saturn, Asc. 7° Scorpio with Uranus. These three are related by similar conditions but on examination the precise details differ.